VISUAL QUICKSTART GUIDE

ADOBE ACROBAT 8

FOR WINDOWS AND MACINTOSH

John Deubert

Peachpit Press

Visual QuickStart Guide
Adobe Acrobat 8 for Windows and Macintosh
John Deubert

Peachpit Press

1249 Eighth Street
Berkeley, CA 94710
(800) 283-9444
(510) 524-2178
(510) 524-2221 (fax)

Find us on the World Wide Web at: www.peachpit.com
To report errors, please send a note to errata@peachpit.com

Peachpit Press is a division of Pearson Education

Editor: Becky Morgan
Production Coordinator: Myrna Vladic
Copyeditor: Tiffany Taylor
Composition: Jerry Ballew
Indexer: Julie Bess
Cover Design: Peachpit Press

ISBN: 0-321-47079-6
9 8 7 6 5 4 3 2

Printed and bound in the United States of America

Dedication

For Barbara, of course.

Acknowledgements

It takes a whole hamlet to write a book and to list everyone who turned a random collection of words into a published volume is probably impossible. However, there are some noteworthy citizens whom I would particularly like to thank. First of all, Becky Morgan, my editor, has a wonderfully gentle way of telling me that my prose has become gibberish, my illustrations are upsetting, and my captions seem copied from an old Bogotá telephone book; thank you very much. Many thanks to Production Editor Myrna Vladic for her tolerance in my unfortunate way with screen shots and naming conventions. (I still feel guilty about the naming convention thing.) Thanks to copyeditor Tiffany Taylor, who ensured my words at least roughly corresponded to the English language and to compositor Jerry Ballew, who managed to somehow place everything on the pages in a pleasing manner. And finally, thanks to indexer Julie Bess who has a job not for the faint of heart. There are undoubtedly other people, whose names I don't know, who made this volume come about; I thank them all.

At home, I thank my wife for her tolerance of my turning for several weeks into He Who Types and Occasionally Eats; she had great patience for an inert husband whose only signs of life were moving fingers. And thanks to granddaughter Elizabeth, who periodically insisted I chase her around the house; some days it was the only exercise I got.

TABLE OF CONTENTS

TABLE OF CONTENTS

STARTING WITH ACROBAT

We'll start with the basics: how to open Acrobat, what you'll be looking at when you do so, and how to quit the application. You'll also learn how to customize some of the Acrobat user interface to your taste.

We'll explore the details and use of Acrobat's toolbars, menus, and other interface items throughout this book; here, we'll orient you so you become comfortable with the layout of the software's windows.

Opening and Quitting Acrobat 8

You open and quit Adobe Acrobat 8 the way you open or close any application on the Macintosh or Windows.

To open Acrobat 8:

◆ Do one of the following:

 ▲ Double-click the Acrobat 8 application icon (**Figure 1.1**).

 ▲ Double-click a PDF file icon.

 ▲ In Windows, choose Acrobat 8 in the Start menu's Programs submenu.

 In all three cases, Acrobat 8 launches. If you double-clicked a PDF file icon, Acrobat presents you with that document's first page.

To quit Acrobat 8:

◆ Do one of the following:

 ▲ On the Macintosh, choose Acrobat > Quit Acrobat.

 ▲ In Windows, choose File > Exit.

 ▲ On either platform, press Command/ Ctrl-Q.

Figure 1.1 Launch Acrobat 8 by clicking either the application or a PDF document icon.

Examining the Getting Started Window

The first window you see when you launch Acrobat 8 is the Getting Started window (**Figure 1.2**). This is a part of Acrobat's help section whose purpose is to introduce you to the many features of Adobe Acrobat.

continues on next page

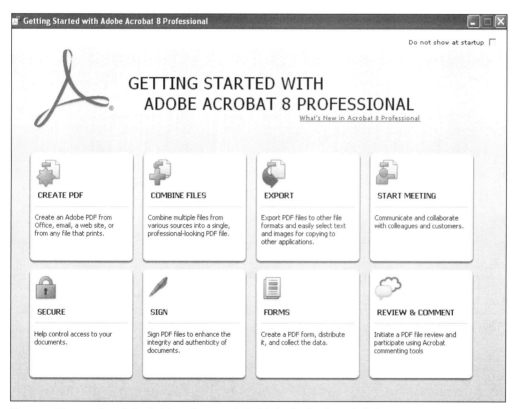

Figure 1.2 When you launch Acrobat 8, you're presented with the Getting Started window.

The Getting Started window presents you with a set of buttons that link to information on a variety of topics regarding significant Acrobat features. When you click one of these buttons, you will be looking at a topic window, similar to that in **Figure 1.3**.

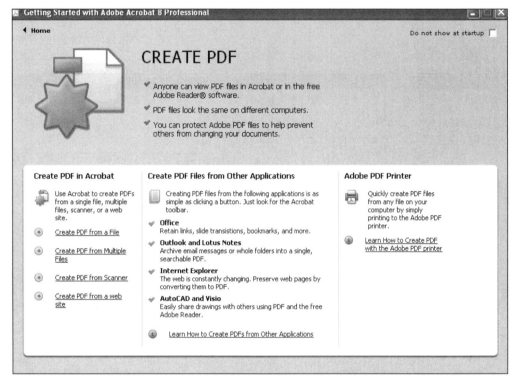

Figure 1.3 A Getting Started Topic window contains links that provide information or carry out a task.

The contents of a Getting Started topic window fall into three categories:

- **Informational text and pictures.** This is often text that describes the benefits of Acrobat features. In Figure 1.3, this includes the box labeled "Create PDF Files from Other Applications.".

- **Links to help topics.** The text associated with these links start with "Learn more," such as the link at the end of the "Adobe PDF Printer" section in Figure 1.3.

- **Links that invoke an Acrobat feature.** These links tell Acrobat to do something. For example, the links in the "Create PDF in Acrobat" section take you to Acrobat tools that create PDFs.

You'll want to explore the topics in this window while you're new to Acrobat; it's an extremely helpful boost to learning Acrobat's features.

✔ Tip

- The Getting Started window will be unnecessary (and annoying) once you become familiar with Acrobat. If you choose the "Do not show at startup" check box, Acrobat will stop automatically displaying this window. You can always get it back by selecting Help > Getting Started.

EXAMINING THE GETTING STARTED WINDOW

Examining the Initial Screen

When you open a document in Acrobat (you'll see how to do this in Chapter 2), you see a window similar to **Figure 1.4**. The parts of this window are as follows:

Drag bar. This is a standard Macintosh or Windows drag bar. In it are all the controls you'll find in any application's document window, including the Close, Minimize, and Zoom buttons.

Document pane. This is where Acrobat displays the pages of your PDF document.

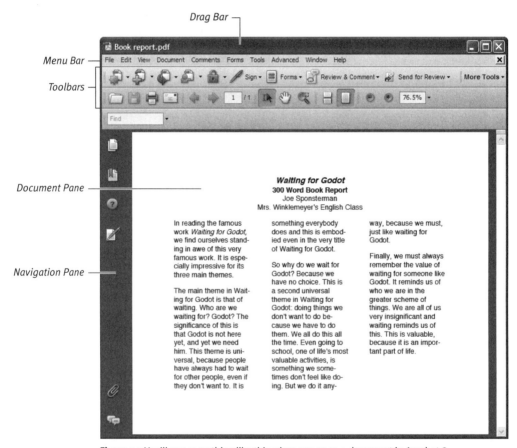

Figure 1.4 You'll see something like this when you open a document in Acrobat 8.

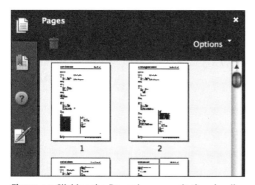

Figure 1.5 Clicking the Pages icon reveals thumbnails of the document's pages.

Menu bar. The location of the menu bar conforms to your platform's standards. In Windows, the menu bar is at the top of the document window, as shown in Figure 1.4; on the Macintosh, the menu bar runs along the top of the screen, as usual.

Toolbars. In Acrobat 8, each document window has its own collection of toolbars. You may customize the exact set of toolbars that is visible and the contents and location of each toolbar; you'll see how to do this shortly.

Navigation panes. This is a series of icons that, when clicked, reveal a variety of tools and information, such as thumbnails of all the pages (as in **Figure 1.5**), all the document's comments, and bookmarks to locations within the document.

✔ Tip

- The drag bar's Close button behaves differently on the Macintosh and Windows. On the Macintosh, the Close button closes the document window but doesn't exit the Acrobat application; in Windows, if no other documents are open, then the Close button closes the document and also exits Acrobat. These are standard behaviors on the Macintosh and in Windows.

Examining the Menus

Acrobat has 10 menus stretching the width of each document window in Windows; it has 11 menus spanning the screen on the Macintosh (**Figure 1.6**). You'll eventually be using items from every one of these menus. For the moment, let's see what these menus are and what kinds of tasks they make possible:

Acrobat menu. This Macintosh-only menu contains items that affect the operation of the application as a whole. In particular, this is where you set the application preferences and exit Acrobat on the Macintosh.

File menu. This menu contains commands to open, close, save, and otherwise manipulate the PDF files on your computer's hard disk. This menu is similar to the File menu in other applications. In Windows, this is where you exit the application.

Edit menu. This is a reasonably standard Macintosh or Windows Edit menu, containing Cut, Copy, Paste, and other common commands. In Windows, this is where you set the application preferences.

View menu. The commands in this menu allow you to change how Acrobat presents your documents. You may choose such things as page display and zoom level. This is also where you can specify which toolbars and navigation panes are visible.

Document menu. Here you may choose commands that manipulate the document's structure, delete or rearrange pages, add headers and footers.

| Acrobat | File | Edit | View | Document | Comments | Forms | Tools | Advanced | Window | Help |

Figure 1.6 The Acrobat menu bar provides access to all the capabilities of the application.

Comments menu. Here are all the commands you'll use in commenting on a PDF document and reading the comments of others.

Forms menu. The items in this menu allow you to create and distribute interactive forms.

Tools menu. This menu contains a set of submenus that provide menu access to features that otherwise are available only through toolbars, such as creating articles or measuring areas and lengths of items on a page. Other submenus enable features important to specific professions, such as prepress.

Advanced menu. The features available through this menu will be used mostly by advanced users. This menu lets you do such things as create a searchable index spanning a collection of PDF files and preflight a document.

Window menu. This menu allows you to specify the details of document windows. You can do such things as tile or stack the windows, bring a particular document to the front, and choose a zoom level.

Help menu. This menu provides access to Acrobat's extensive help system, which includes a full Acrobat reference and the Getting Started window. It also lets you check for updates and register your Acrobat software.

EXAMING THE MENUS

Examining the Toolbars

Acrobat 8 has a very large number of toolbars that supply access to the application's many features (**Figure 1.7**).

One change in the user interface from previous Acrobat versions is that each document window in Acrobat 8 has a copy of all the currently visible toolbars, rather than having a single set of toolbars available to the application as a whole.

Most of Acrobat's toolbars aren't initially visible. Showing a toolbar and then hiding it again entails the simple selection of a menu item.

All the toolbars may be "torn off" the document window to become standalone palettes.

To make a toolbar visible:

1. Choose a toolbar in the View > Toolbars submenu (**Figure 1.8**).

   Acrobat makes the toolbar visible as a stand-alone palette (**Figure 1.9**).

2. If you want the toolbar docked, drag the palette to the collection of toolbars at the top of a document window. (We talk more about toolbars and palettes next.)

   Acrobat adds the palette to the window as a toolbar.

✔ Tip

■ You may want to leave the toolbar in its palette form; this is useful if you're going to use the toolbar only once and then hide it again.

Figure 1.7 Acrobat 8 toolbars are fixed to document windows.

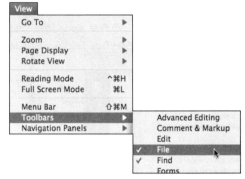

Figure 1.8 You specify the toolbars you want visible by selecting them in the Toolbars submenu.

Figure 1.9 Toolbars may be displayed as stand-alone palettes. Here is the File toolbar.

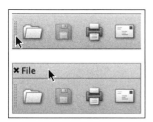

Figure 1.10 The vertical dotted lines at the left of a toolbar are the drag area.

To convert a toolbar into a palette:

1. Click and hold toolbar's *drag area*.

This is the pair of vertical dotted lines at the left edge of each toolbar, indicated in the top image of **Figure 1.10**.

2. Drag the toolbar off the collection of tool-bars at the top of the document window.

Acrobat converts the toolbar into a palette, as in the bottom image of Figure 1.10.

To convert a palette into a toolbar:

1. Click and hold the drag bar at the top of the palette, as in the bottom of Figure 1.10.

2. Drag the palette onto the toolbar in the position you want for the resulting toolbar.

Acrobat adds the palette to the toolbar.

Acrobat 8 toolbars

◆ **Advanced Editing.** Contains tools for advanced Acrobat features, such as placing movies and adding links on a page.

◆ **Comment & Markup toolbar.** Tools for adding comments to a page.

◆ **Edit toolbar.** The tools here allow you to perform a variety of tasks that change the contents of the page: add articles and links, crop, and place movies, and other actions that modify the page.

◆ **File toolbar.** Tools to open, close, and otherwise work with files available to your computer.

◆ **Find toolbar.** This contains a text field you may use to search in the current document.

◆ **Forms toolbar.** This contains tools for adding interactive form fields to your document.

EXAMINING THE TOOLBARS

- **Measuring toolbar.** This contains tools that let you measure the size and area of objects in your document.

- **Object Data toolbar.** This toolbar contains a single tool that lets you view object data associated with an image or artwork with Microsoft Visio.

- **Page Display toolbar.** This toolbar lets you specify whether Acrobat should display your pages one at a time or as a scrolling column of pages.

- **Page Navigation toolbar.** Here are the controls that let you move from page to page within your document.

- **Print Production toolbar.** This contains a number of tools with features important to professional printing.

- **Redaction toolbar.** These tools let you mark sensitive text within your document for hiding or removal.

- **Select & Zoom toolbar.** Contains the most-routinely used tools: the Hand, Selection, and Zoom tools.

- **Tasks toolbar.** Here are a set of drop down menus that allow convenient access to frequent tasks, such as creating a PDF or accessing commenting tools.

- **Typewriter toolbar.** This toolbar has tools that let you fill in a scanned paper form without explicitly adding PDF form fields to the document.

- **Properties bar.** Not properly a toolbar, the Properties bar presents information that is useful when you are creating links, form fields, and other objects within Acrobat.

EXAMINING THE TOOLBARS

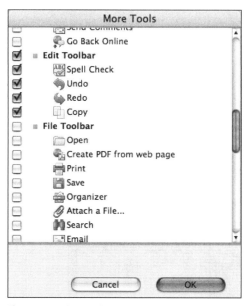

Figure 1.11 Select or deselect each of the tools to make them visible or hidden in Acrobat's toolbars.

Customizing Toolbars

You can control which tools appear in a toolbar. Each toolbar has a set of tool buttons associated with it, and you can choose which of these buttons are visible. The new collection of toolbars you specify will appear in every new document window you open from now on.

To add or remove toolbar tools:

1. Select View > Toolbars > More Tools.

   Acrobat displays the More Tools dialog box (**Figure 1.11**). This dialog box displays all the tools that can appear in each of the toolbars.

2. Select the check box next to each of the tools that you want visible in your toolbars.

3. Deselect the check box next to each of the tools that you don't want visible.

4. Click OK.

✔ Tip

- A couple of common tools are inexplicably missing in the default setup of their corresponding toolbars. I strongly recommend that you enable the following tools: in the Select & Zoom toolbar, Actual Size, Fit Width, and Fit Page; in the Page Navigation toolbar, Next View and Previous View.

Toolbar Philosophy

People differ in their philosophies regarding toolbars. Some people like to have a toolbar button for every command of which the application is capable. On the other hand, I prefer to have toolbar buttons for only those commands that I use a lot and that are inconvenient to invoke with the keyboard.

The nice thing about Acrobat 8 is that it allows you to set things up just the way you like.

Working with Navigation Panes

The navigation panes occupy an area along the left side of every document window. Normally, the panes are retracted, showing only a column of icons called *tabs* in Acrobat parlance, one for each available pane (**Figure 1.12**). When a pane is opened, it allows you to move around within your document in a specific way, such as moving from page to page using thumbnails, moving among the document's bookmarks, and so on (as shown earlier in Figure 1.4).

To open and close a navigation pane:

1. Click the tab of a closed navigation pane to open it.

   Acrobat opens the navigation pane (**Figure 1.13**).

2. Click the tab of an open pane to close it again.

   The navigation pane collapses down into a tab.

Acrobat defines a large number of navigation panes that may be available to the user. Most of them aren't initially visible; Acrobat starts out showing only the most commonly used panes.

It's easy to choose which panes Acrobat should make available in document windows so that you have convenient access to them.

To customize the list of navigation panes:

◆ Choose the pane you want to make visible in the View > Navigation Panels submenu (**Figure 1.14**).

   Acrobat will toggle the visibility of the navigation tab you choose; if it was visible, it will become hidden, and vice versa.

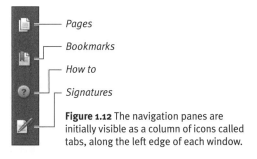

Pages

Bookmarks

How to

Signatures

Figure 1.12 The navigation panes are initially visible as a column of icons called tabs, along the left edge of each window.

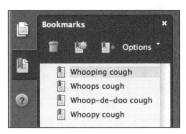

Figure 1.13 Clicking one of the navigation tabs exposes the pane associated with that tab.

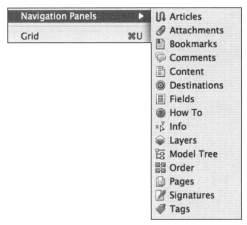

Figure 1.14 The Navigation Panels submenu allows you to toggle the visibility of navigation panes.

Figure 1.15 All the navigation tabs may be converted to stand-alone palettes.

Acrobat 8 navigation panes

Many of the navigation panes have a somewhat specialized purpose, and won't be covered in this book. Here we'll list the navigation panes that are most useful:

Articles. Lists all the articles that exist in the document. Articles are a useful tool for making documents readable; we'll discuss them in Chapter 10.

Bookmarks. Lists all the bookmarks placed in the document. These form a clickable table of contents for the PDF file. In Chapter 10, you'll see how to make and use bookmarks.

Comments. Lists all the annotations that have been placed on pages in the document.

How to. Part of the Acrobat help system, which steps you through carrying out certain tasks.

Pages. Presents thumbnail views of each page in the document. Double-clicking a thumbnail takes you to that page.

Signatures. Lists all of the document's electronic signatures.

Any of the navigation panes may be converted to a stand-alone palette, as in **Figure 1.15**.

To convert a navigation pane into a palette:

◆ Click and drag the pane's tab away from the left edge of the window.

Acrobat converts the pane into a palette.

To convert a palette into a navigation pane:

◆ Click and drag the palette into the navigation pane area of a document window.

Acrobat converts the palette into a navigation pane.

WORKING WITH NAVIGATION PANES

Setting Preferences

As is true of all applications, Acrobat maintains a set of preferences that determine how the application should behave when you start a session. This can include such things as the default zoom, the color to be used for comments, and whether Acrobat should report distances in pixels, inches, or centimeters. Some of the tasks in this book require you to set preferences relevant to that task. In the meantime, you may find it useful to look at the preference controls available in Acrobat. (There are a lot of them.)

To set Acrobat's preferences:

1. On the Macintosh, choose Acrobat > Preferences. In Windows, choose Edit > Preferences

    Acrobat will display the Preferences dialog box (**Figure 1.16**).

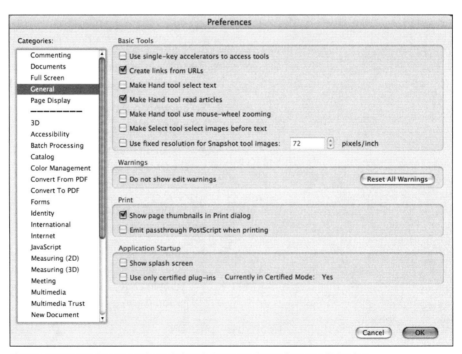

Figure 1.16 You can change Acrobat's default behavior in the Preferences dialog box.

2. Click the category name in the list running down the left side of the dialog box.

Acrobat presents the controls that apply to that category.

3. Make whatever changes you wish to the preferences controls in that category.

Repeat steps 2 and 3 for as many categories as you want.

4. Click OK.

✔ Tip

■ In your idle moments, you should browse the preference controls available in the Preferences dialog box. It may not sound entertaining, but you'll be surprised how much you can learn about an application's capabilities from the preference controls it provides.

SETTING PREFERENCES

VIEWING A
DOCUMENT

Once you've launched Acrobat and have become familiar with its interface, you're ready to navigate among the pages of an open document. This chapter will describe the tools in Acrobat that you use to view a PDF document. We'll look at some routine things, such as all the ways to move from page to page and how to zoom in and out, as well as some of Acrobat's more exotic capabilities, such as measuring the length and area of items on the page.

Opening a PDF File

Arguably, the most basic activity you can carry out in Acrobat is opening a PDF file. You can do this several ways, most of them identical to the way you open files in other applications.

To open a file from the Finder or Windows Explorer:

◆ Do either of the following:

▲ Double-click the icon of a PDF file.

or

▲ Drag the icon of a PDF file to the Acrobat application icon.

Acrobat opens the file.

To open a file from the File menu:

1. Choose File > Open (Command/Ctrl-O) (**Figure 2.1**).

Acrobat will present you with the standard select-a-file dialog box.

2. Navigate to the file you want to open, and click OK.

Acrobat opens the file.

To open a file from the File toolbar:

1. Display the File toolbar, if necessary, by selecting View > Toolbars > File.

Acrobat displays the File toolbar (**Figure 2.2**).

2. Click the Open File icon in the File toolbar.

The standard select-a-file dialog box opens.

3. Choose the file you want to open, and click OK.

Acrobat opens the file.

Figure 2.1 You can open a PDF file in Acrobat by selecting File > Open.

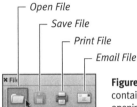

Open File
Save File
Print File
Email File

Figure 2.2 The File toolbar contains handy tools for opening and saving files.

Figure 2.3 The Page Navigation toolbar contains the following tools: Previous Page, Next Page, and a Page Number text box.

Figure 2.4 Move to an arbitrary page by double-clicking a thumbnail in the Pages navigation pane.

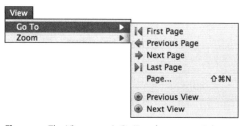

Figure 2.5 The View menu's Go To submenu contains useful commands that let you navigate among pages.

Moving from Page to Page

Having opened your document, you'll want to move around among the pages. Here, too, there are several ways to do so, most of them familiar from other applications.

To move to the next or previous page:

◆ Do one of the following:

▲ Press the right or left arrow key on your keyboard to move to the next or previous page, respectively.

▲ Click the Previous or Next Page tool in the Page Navigation toolbar (**Figure 2.3**).

▲ Press the Page Down or Page Up key on your keyboard.

To move to a particular page:

◆ Do one of the following:

▲ Type the page number to which you want to go in the Page Number field in the Page Navigation toolbar (Figure 2.3).

▲ Click the Pages navigation tab to expose the Pages navigation pane, and then double-click the thumbnail of your desired page (**Figure 2.4**).

To move to the first or last page:

1. To go to the document's first page, select View > Go To > First Page (**Figure 2.5**) or press the Home key.

2. To go to the document's last page, select View > Go To > Last Page or press the End key.

✔ Tip

■ You can add tools to the Page Navigation toolbar for First Page and Last Page. I recommend you do so; they are very handy. Chapter 1 tells you how to add tools to a toolbar.

Moving from View to View

A *view* in Acrobat parlance is a combination of document, page number, and zoom. You change to a new view whenever you go to a new page, zoom in or out, or open a new document.

Acrobat has menu items and associated key shortcuts for moving to the previous and next views. If you jump ahead 15 pages by double-clicking a thumbnail, the Previous View command returns you to your original page. These controls are very handy.

To move to the previous or next view:

◆ Do one of the following:
  ▲ Select View > Go To > Previous View or View > Go To > Next View (Figure 2.5).
  ▲ Press Command/Ctrl-left arrow key or Command/Ctrl-right arrow key on your keyboard.

✔ Tip

■ I recommend that you add to the Page Navigation toolbar the tools for First and Last Page and for Next and Previous View (**Figure 2.6**). These functions are so frequently used that you'll want to make access to them as convenient as possible. Chapter 1 tells you how to add tools to a toolbar.

Figure 2.6 You can add to the Page Navigation toolbar tools for First and Last Page and for Next and Previous View.

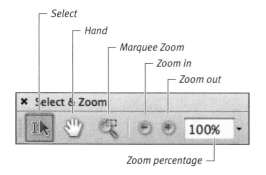

Figure 2.7 The Zoom toolbar contains all the tools you need to zoom in and out of your PDFs.

Zooming In and Out

Acrobat provides a Select & Zoom toolbar (**Figure 2.7**) with tools that let you get a closer look at an area of the page or to look at a broader region of the page.

In Acrobat's default configuration, the Select & Zoom toolbar contains the zoom tools you will use most often. Acrobat's menus also offer less-frequently used zoom functions.

The zoom tools have three broad classes of functionality. You can do any of the following:

◆ Zoom by a specific amount.

◆ Zoom so that the page fits in the document window in a particular way (for example, the page width fills the window).

◆ Dynamically select the degree of zoom visually.

✔ Tip

■ You can add the additional zoom tools to the Zoom toolbar. **Figure 2.8** shows the Zoom toolbar fully loaded with all the zoom tools. See Chapter 1 for a reminder of how to add tools to a toolbar.

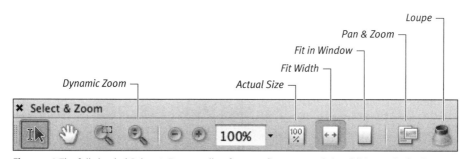

Figure 2.8 The fully loaded Select & Zoom toolbar features five more tools in addition to the basic ones.

To zoom by a fixed amount:

◆ Do one of the following:

▲ Click the Zoom In tool on the Select & Zoom toolbar.

Acrobat zooms in to a predetermined zoom level. For example, starting at 100%, repeated clicks of the + button take you to zooms of 125%, 150%, 200%, and so on in intervals up to 6400%.

▲ Type a zoom percentage in the Select & Zoom toolbar's text box.

▲ Click the small, downward arrowhead next to the Select & Zoom toolbar's text box, and select a predefined zoom amount from the resulting Zoom Amount menu (**Figure 2.9**).

▲ Choose Actual Size in the Zoom Amount menu, or press Command/ Ctrl-1 to zoom to 100%.

To zoom the page to fit the document window:

◆ Do one of the following:

▲ Choose Fit Page from the Zoom Amount menu on the Select & Zoom toolbar or press Command/Ctrl-0 to zoom out until the page fits entirely inside the document window (**Figure 2.10**).

▲ Choose Fit Width from the Zoom Amount menu or press Command/ Ctrl-2 to zoom in until the document's pages exactly fit the width of the window (Figure 2.10).

▲ Choose Fit Height from the Zoom Amount menu to zoom until the document's pages exactly fit the height of the window.

▲ Choose Fit Visible from the Zoom Amount menu or press Command/ Ctrl-3 to zoom until the text and images on your pages exactly fit the document window.

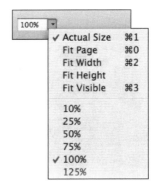

Figure 2.9 The drop-down menu in the Select & Zoom toolbar lets you conveniently choose a zoom amount.

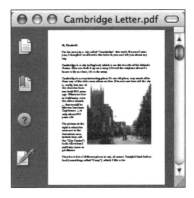

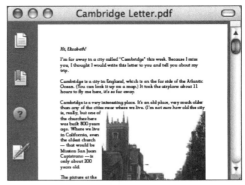

Figure 2.10 Two useful zoom amounts are Fit Page (top) and Fit Width.

ZOOMING IN AND OUT

Figure 2.11 When you use the Marquee Zoom tool, the mouse pointer normally is a magnifying glass with a plus sign. You can zoom out (and change the point pointer to a minus sign) by holding the Shift key.

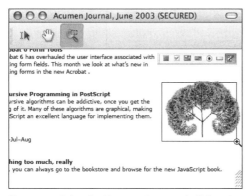

Figure 2.12 Using the Marquee Zoom tool, click and drag a rectangle.

Figure 2.13 Acrobat zooms in until the rectangle fills the window.

Figure 2.14 The Tools > Select & Zoom submenu contains items for the Marquee Zoom and Dynamic Zoom tools.

The Marquee Zoom tool

The Marquee Zoom tool is the best tool to use when you want to get a better look at a particular part of the page.

To zoom with the Marquee Zoom tool:

1. In the Select & Zoom toolbar, click the Marquee Zoom tool.

   The mouse pointer turns into a magnifying glass with a plus sign in it (**Figure 2.11**).

2. Click in the document window, and drag a rectangle around the area to which you want to zoom (**Figure 2.12**).

   Acrobat zooms in until the area you enclosed in the marquee fills the document window (**Figure 2.13**).

✔ Tips

- If you click in the document window without dragging a rectangle, Acrobat zooms in by a predefined amount. The point on which you clicked is centered on the resulting, zoomed page.

- The Marquee Zoom tool can be used to zoom out of the page, as well. Repeat the steps in the previous task while holding down the Shift key. Instead of zooming in, Acrobat zooms out, showing you more of the page.

- You can get temporary access to the Marquee Zoom tool at any time by holding down Command/Ctrl-Spacebar on your keyboard. Acrobat will activate the Marquee Zoom feature, allowing you to zoom in on the page. If you also hold down the Alt/Option key (Command-Option-Space/Ctrl-Alt-Space) you'll be temporarily able to zoom out.

- If the Basic toolbar isn't visible, you can get to the Marquee Zoom tool by selecting Tools > Select & Zoom > Marquee Zoom (**Figure 2.14**).

ZOOMING IN AND OUT

The Dynamic Zoom tool

The Dynamic Zoom tool allows you to zoom in and out of your document page by clicking and moving your mouse. Dragging the mouse to the upper left zooms in to the document; dragging to the lower right zooms out (**Figure 2.15**).

Figure 2.15 The Dynamic Zoom tool allows you to zoom in and out of your document by clicking and dragging your mouse.

To zoom using the Dynamic Zoom tool:

1. Select Tools > Select & Zoom > Dynamic Zoom (Figure 2.14).

   The mouse pointer changes to the cursor shown in **Figure 2.16**.

2. Click and hold the mouse button anywhere in the document window.

Figure 2.16 The mouse pointer looks like this with the Dynamic Zoom tool active.

3. Drag up and to the left to zoom in on the document.

4. Drag down and to the right to zoom out.

Figure 2.17 The Loupe tool lets you drag a target rectangle around the page and view a close-up of the rectangle's contents in a dialog box.

The Loupe tool

The Loupe tool gives you a close-up of the area on the screen surrounding the mouse pointer. As you move the pointer around the document window, a floating loupe window shows a continually updating close-up.

Unfortunately, this useful tool does not appear on the Select & Zoom toolbar by default. You must select it in the Tools > Select & Zoom submenu (Figure 2.14). You can, of course, add it to the Select & Zoom toolbar using the procedure described in Chapter 1.

To zoom with the Loupe tool:

1. Select Tools > Select & Zoom > Loupe Tool.

   The mouse pointer changes to a small crosshair shape.

2. Click in the document window.

   Acrobat displays a *target rectangle* in the document window and a floating Loupe Tool window that shows a close-up of whatever is in the rectangle (**Figure 2.17**).

   You can drag this rectangle around the document window to see different parts of the page.

   Note in Figure 2.17 that the Loupe Tool floating window has controls that let you specify such things as the degree of magnification and the color of the target rectangle.

The Pan & Zoom tool

Acrobat's final zoom tool is Pan & Zoom. This is the opposite of the Loupe tool. Acrobat presents you with a floating window containing a thumbnail view of your page. You drag and resize a target rectangle in the thumbnail, and Acrobat zooms the main document page so that the target rectangle fills the page.

Like the Loupe tool, the Pan & Zoom tool is initially available only through the Tools > Select & Zoom submenu (Figure 2.14). You can add it to the Select & Zoom toolbar, as described in Chapter 1.

To zoom with the Pan & Zoom tool:

1. Select Tools > Select & Zoom > Pan & Zoom Window.

   Acrobat displays a floating Pan & Zoom window containing a thumbnail image of your document page. The floating window also has a target rectangle initially set to encompass the entire page (**Figure 2.18**).

2. Resize and move the target rectangle so that it encloses the area on the thumbnail that you want to see close up.

   As you do so, Acrobat continuously zooms the document window so that it's filled with the area enclosed by the target rectangle (**Figure 2.19**).

   You resize the rectangle by grabbing handles that appear at its corners and sides when the mouse pointer rolls over it.

   If you wish, you can use the controls on the Pan & Zoom thumbnail window to select an explicit scale, change the color of the target rectangle, or move from page to page within the document.

Figure 2.18 When you click the Pan & Zoom tool, Acrobat presents you with a floating thumbnail view of your page enclosed in a "target rectangle."

Figure 2.19 As you move and resize the target rectangle, Acrobat zooms the main document window so the rectangle's contents fill the window.

ZOOMING IN AND OUT

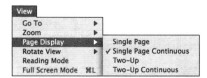

Figure 2.20 You select a page layout from the View > Page Display submenu.

Figure 2.21 Two layouts are available by default in the Page Display toolbar.

Figure 2.22 Two of the layouts available are Single Page and Single Page Continuous.

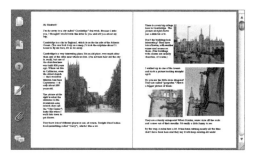

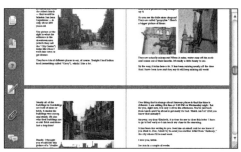

Figure 2.23 The Two-Up (top) and Two-Up Continuous (bottom) layouts are useful for seeing how printed documents will look when the pages are bound.

Selecting a Page Layout

Acrobat can organize your document's pages on the screen a number of ways, such as one page at a time or side by side. These layouts are available from the View > Page Display submenu (**Figure 2.20**); some of them are available by default from the Page Display toolbar (**Figure 2.21**) as well.

To change the page layout:

◆ Do one of the following:

▲ Select the desired layout from View > Page Display.

▲ Click the layout button in the Page Display toolbar.

By default, only two layouts—Single Page and Single Page Continuous— are available in this toolbar. You can add the other layouts to the toolbar; see Chapter 1 for instructions on how to customize a toolbar.

Acrobat page layouts

The Page Display submenu allows you access to the following layouts:

◆ **Single Page** displays one page at a time in the document window (**Figure 2.22**).

◆ **Single Page Continuous** displays the pages in the document as a single, scrollable column (Figure 2.22).

◆ **Two-Up** displays two pages at a time, side by side (**Figure 2.23**).

◆ **Two-Up Continuous** displays two columns of side-by-side pages (Figure 2.23).

✔ Tip

■ The Two-Up and Two-Up Continuous layouts are particularly useful for PDF files that are intended to be bound in a book; they allow you to see how the pages will look when the book is open.

SELECTING A PAGE LAYOUT

Searching for Text

Acrobat has an effective mechanism for searching for a particular piece of text within a document. It's similar to the Search features in other applications.

Acrobat has two distinct mechanisms for finding text in a document:

Find looks for text within the current document. Acrobat lets you step through successive instances of the found text one at a time.

Search looks for text in one or more PDF files in locations you specify on your computer's disk. Acrobat presents you with a clickable list of all the instances of that text within the documents.

To find text in a document:

1. If the Find toolbar isn't visible, select Edit > Find (Command/Ctrl-F).

   Acrobat makes the Find toolbar visible (**Figure 2.24**).

2. Type into the text field the word or phrase you want to find.

3. Press the Enter/Return key.

   Acrobat searches the document for the text, stops when it finds an instance, and highlights the text on the page (**Figure 2.25**).

4. To go to the next instance of the text in the document, click the Find Next button on the Find toolbar.

5. To go to the previous instance of the text, click the Find Previous button.

✔ Tip

■ The Find feature ignores case and diacritical marks in its search; that is, *José* and *jose* are considered identical.

Figure 2.24 The Find toolbar has a text field for the text you want to find, a Find Previous button, and a Find Next button.

> *Waiting for Godot*
> **300 Word Book Report**
> Joe Sponsterman
> Mrs. Winklemeyer's English Class

Figure 2.25 When the Find function discovers an instance of the word, it moves the document window so the word is visible and highlights the text on the page.

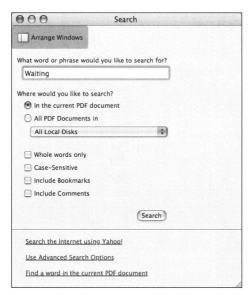

Figure 2.26 The Search dialog box allows you to search for a word or phrase in all of the PDF files in a particular location.

Figure 2.27 The Locations pop-up menu in the Search dialog box lets you specify where Acrobat should look for PDF files to search.

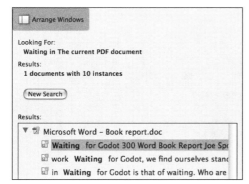

Figure 2.28 The Search feature returns a list of all of the instances it finds. Click one of the instances to see the page on which it resides.

To search for text in one or more documents:

1. Select Edit > Search, or press Command/ Ctrl-Shift-F.

    The Search dialog box opens (**Figure 2.26**).

2. Type into the text box the word or phrase for which you want to search.

3. Use the two radio buttons to specify where Acrobat should search for the text: in the current PDF document or in all PDF documents in a particular location.

    In the latter case, you may choose a location from the pop-up menu (**Figure 2.27**).

4. Select the check boxes associated with the options you want for the search:

    ▲ **Whole words only**—Acrobat ignores the text if it's preceded or followed by other alphanumeric characters. Thus, in searching for *wait*, Acrobat ignores *waiting*.

    ▲ **Case-Sensitive**—Acrobat considers case in its search; thus, *Wait* and *wait* are considered different.

    ▲ **Include Bookmarks**—Acrobat searches the titles of the document's bookmarks as well as page contents.

    ▲ **Include Comments**—Acrobat searches comments.

5. Click the Search button.

    Acrobat searches all the documents for the specified text. It then creates a list showing all the instances it finds (**Figure 2.28**).

6. To examine any of the found instances, click that instance in the list.

    The document window will show you the found text, opening a new PDF file if that is where the text resides.

7. Click the New Search button to start a new search, or click the dialog box's Close button to close the Search dialog box.

Arranging Documents on the Screen

Acrobat lets you tile or cascade the currently open document windows. When you choose one of these options, the document windows are resized so that your entire screen is filled.

All of these options are available through the Window menu (**Figure 2.29**).

To arrange documents on the screen:

◆ Do one of the following:

▲ Select Window > Cascade.

Acrobat zooms the document windows to full-screen, offset so that the title bars of the rear windows are all visible (**Figure 2.30**).

▲ Select Window > Tile > Vertically.

Acrobat tiles the windows top to bottom (**Figure 2.31**).

▲ Select Window > Tile > Horizontally.

Acrobat tiles the windows across the width of the page.

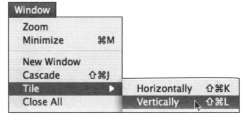

Figure 2.29 You can tile or cascade open document windows by selecting the appropriate items in the Window menu.

Figure 2.30 Cascading the document windows is useful when you want to see only one of them at a time.

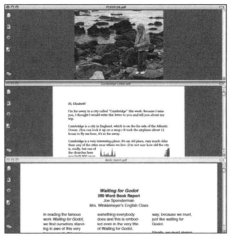

Figure 2.31 Tiling the windows is helpful when you want all the documents to be visible simultaneously for comparison.

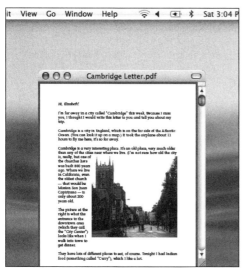

Figure 2.32 In Reading mode, Acrobat hides the toolbar and navigation tabs and zooms the document so that its width stretches across the window.

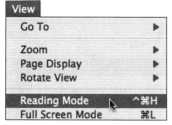

Figure 2.33 Enter Reading mode using the View menu.

Using Reading Mode

Reading mode is new to Acrobat 8. When in Reading mode, Acrobat hides the toolbars and navigation tabs and zooms the document so that it fits across the width of the document window (**Figure 2.32**). Additionally, each click of the mouse moves you down the document by one screen.

✔ Tip

■ Reading mode is particularly useful for reading documents that were originally formatted for print. It makes it easy to read the small text used in such documents.

To enter and exit Reading mode:

1. To enter Reading mode, select View > Reading Mode (**Figure 2.33**).

   When you click the page in Reading mode, Acrobat advances your page by a screen or to the next page, whichever is appropriate.

2. To exit Reading mode, choose View > Reading Mode, or press the Escape key.

To navigate pages in Reading mode:

1. To move forward in the document, do one of the following:
   - ▲ Press the right arrow key on your keyboard.

     Acrobat takes you to the next page.
   - ▲ Click with the mouse on the page.

     Acrobat takes you forward one screen or to the next page, whichever is shorter.

continues on next page

2. To move backward through the document, do one of the following:

▲ Press the left arrow key on your keyboard.

Acrobat takes you to the previous page.

▲ Shift-click with the mouse on the page.

Acrobat takes you backward one screen or to the previous page, whichever is shorter.

✔ Tips

■ In Reading mode, the mouse pointer turns into a hand with an arrow in it (**Figure 2.34**). This pointer always indicates that clicking the mouse will move your view forward or back in the document.

■ Reading mode is much like Full Screen mode. It hides extraneous controls, toolbars, and other distractions; it also automatically moves ahead in the document with a click of the mouse button. Reading mode, however, leaves you with access to the rest of your computer; you can click outside the document window to look briefly at your email or do some other task. In Full Screen mode, nothing is visible except the PDF document; you must explicitly leave Full Screen mode to do anything else on your computer. We'll talk about Full Screen mode in detail in Chapter 11.

Figure 2.34 In Reading mode, the mouse pointer changes, telling you that mouse clicks will move you to the next or (with Shift) the previous page.

USING READING MODE

Figure 2.35 Links in PDF pages usually look like links on Web pages.

Figure 2.36 A pointing finger indicates that you're over a link.

Using Links and Bookmarks

Acrobat gives the author of a PDF file the ability to add navigation features that make it easy for a reader to move around a document. In Chapter 11, you'll see how to create these navigation features. Here, you'll learn to use these features when viewing a PDF document.

Again, the author must build these features into the PDF document for them to be available to the reader.

Using links

Links in Acrobat work just like links in Web pages. You click them, and the document does something: moves to another location in the document, plays a movie, or performs some other activity determined by the document designer.

It's up to the creator of the PDF file to make a page's links visible to the reader. Again, you see the same range of visual clues that you find on a Web page, such as blue text and button icons (**Figure 2.35**).

✔ Tips

- As in a Web browser, you can always tell when the mouse cursor is over a link because the cursor changes to a pointing finger (**Figure 2.36**).

- The destination associated with a link may be in a different file. Some documents are distributed as a set of PDF files, one for each chapter; clicking a link in the "Table of Contents" file takes you to the file that contains that topic.

USING LINKS AND BOOKMARKS

Using bookmarks

Bookmarks reside in the Bookmarks pane, one of the navigation tabs along the left side of your document windows. They form a clickable table of contents provided by the document's author.

Clicking a bookmark takes you to a predetermined location in the document.

To use a document's bookmarks:

1. Click the Bookmarks navigation tab to open the Bookmarks pane, if necessary.

   You see all of the document's bookmarks (**Figure 2.37**).

2. Click a bookmark.

   Acrobat takes you to the location associated with that bookmark.

Figure 2.37 Clicking the Bookmarks navigation tab exposes the document's bookmarks.

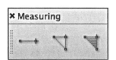

Figure 2.38 The Measuring toolbar contains the Distance, Perimeter, and Area tools.

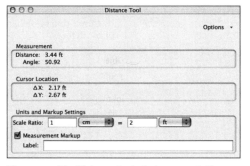

Figure 2.39 The Distance Tool window reports the distance between the two points you specify on the page. Note that Acrobat can translate distance on the screen into real distances using the scale ratio.

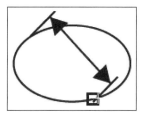

Figure 2.40 After you click once with the Distance tool, Acrobat draws a double-arrow line connecting your original point with the mouse pointer's current position.

Measuring Sizes and Areas

Acrobat provides a set of tools that you can use to measure the sizes and areas of items on a page. These measurements can be reported in any units you wish; you specify a scale (so many millimeters equals so many feet, for example), and Acrobat reports its results in real units. This makes these tools extremely useful for working with maps, floor plans, and other scale drawings.

The tools you'll use to do this are on the Measuring toolbar (**Figure 2.38**).

To measure the distance between two points:

1. Select View > Toolbars > Measuring to make the Measuring toolbar visible, if necessary.

2. Select the Distance tool.

   The mouse pointer becomes a cross-hair, and the Distance Tool floating window opens (**Figure 2.39**).

3. Set the scale of your drawing using the two edit boxes and pop-up menus in the Units and Markup Settings area.

   Acrobat will report distances using this scale. In Figure 2.40, the scale specifies that 1 centimeter equals 2 feet.

4. Click once on the starting point for the distance you want to measure.

   Now, wherever you move your mouse, Acrobat draws a double-arrow line (**Figure 2.40**) that shows the distance between the mouse's current position and the starting point. The Distance Tool window also continually reports the distance from the starting point to the mouse's current position.

continues on next page

5. Click the second endpoint for the distance you want to measure.

The Distance Tool window reports the distance between your endpoints. By default, Acrobat also adds to the page a special annotation called a *measurement markup* (**Figure 2.41**). You may prevent this by unchecking the Measurement Markup check box in the Distance Tool window.

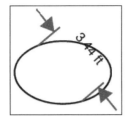

Figure 2.41 The Distance tool, by default, adds a measurement markup annotation to the page. This annotation remains on the page indefinitely; it doesn't disappear when you stop using the Distance tool.

✔ Tips

■ All three measurement tools jump to any line art on the page that is near the mouse pointer. This behavior makes it easy to measure the distance between two drawn items on the document page.

■ Measurement markups are useful if you want the distance or area reported as part of your page. Otherwise, you should turn them off.

■ If you get an unwanted measurement markup on the page (I'm always forgetting to turn off this feature), you can easily remove it by clicking it with the Hand tool or Selection tool (both in the Basic toolbar) and pressing Delete.

MEASURING SIZES AND AREAS

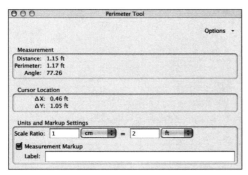

Figure 2.42 The Perimeter Tool window displays the distance around a perimeter you define.

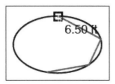

Figure 2.43 As you click around the edge of the region, the Perimeter tool displays a running sum of the perimeter distance so far.

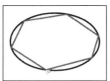

Figure 2.44 The Perimeter tool finishes by adding a measurement markup to your page (the polygon in this illustration).

The Perimeter tool

The Perimeter tool adds the lengths of a series of line segments that you place around the edge of an object or region on the page.

To measure the perimeter of a region:

1. Select the Perimeter tool in the Measuring toolbar.

   The mouse pointer becomes a cross-hair, and Acrobat will display the Perimeter Tool floating window (**Figure 2.42**).

2. Set the scale of your drawing in the Perimeter Tool dialog box.

3. Click at the starting point for the distance you want to measure.

4. Click successively on points around the perimeter of the area you want to measure.

   As you do so, Acrobat shows you the set of straight lines connecting your points as well as a running total of your distance so far (**Figure 2.43**). This distance also appears in the Perimeter Tool window.

5. Click twice on the final point of your perimeter to let Acrobat know you're done.

   Acrobat freezes the values displayed Perimeter Tool dialog box. It also, by default, adds a measurement markup annotation to the page (the polygon shown in **Figure 2.44**). You can turn off this feature in the Perimeter Tool window.

✔ Tip

■ All the measurement tools display a small square near the mouse pointer (clearly visible in Figure 2.44). This square becomes solid black when the mouse pointer is over a path on the PDF page. This makes it easy to be sure you're clicking right on the path you're trying to measure.

The Area tool

The Area tool works identically to the Perimeter tool, except that it reports the area of the enclosed space you map out with your line segments.

To measure the area of a region:

1. Select the Area tool in the Measuring toolbar.

   The mouse pointer becomes a cross-hair, and the Area Tool floating window opens (**Figure 2.45**).

2. Set the scale of your drawing in the Area Tool dialog box.

3. Click at the starting point for the region whose area you want to measure.

4. Click successively on points around the perimeter of the region.

   As you do so, Acrobat shows the set of straight lines connecting your points (**Figure 2.46**). Unlike with the Perimeter tool, there's no running total.

5. Click the starting point to close the region.

   The Area Tool dialog box displays the area of the region enclosed by your line segments. As before, Acrobat adds a measurement markup annotation to the page (**Figure 2.47**), unless you've turned off this feature in the Area Tool window.

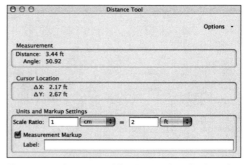

Figure 2.45 The Area Tool floating window displays the area of a region on the page.

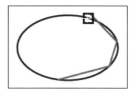

Figure 2.46 Using the Area tool, click around the periphery of the region in which you're interested.

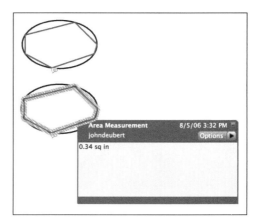

Figure 2.47 The Area tool leaves a measurement markup on the page, unless you've off turned that feature.

SAVING AND
PRINTING FILES

3

A document in your computer's memory is intrinsically impermanent. For your document to trot even a short distance along the sands of time, you need to be able to save it to disk and print it.

Remarkably, Acrobat lets you save your PDF documents to a wide variety of formats. If you need to convert a PDF file to a TIFF file or an EPS file, just select those formats when you save the file.

At print time, Acrobat gives you a lot of control over the details of how your document is placed on paper. You can even make a booklet out of your PDF file directly from Acrobat.

In this chapter, you'll see how to use all of Acrobat's file saving, conversion, and printing capabilities.

Saving a PDF File

Many of the tasks in this book modify documents with which you're working; commenting, touching up text, and adding links all change the file. To make these changes permanent, you must save the file back to your hard disk.

Acrobat does this the same way as most other applications.

To save a document to disk:

◆ Select File > Save.

Acrobat saves the PDF file onto your hard disk with its existing name.

To save a document with a new name:

1. Select File > Save As, or click the Save button on the File toolbar (**Figure 3.1**).

   In either case, a standard Save As dialog box opens (**Figure 3.2**).

2. Navigate to the folder on your disk in which you want to save the file.

3. Type a new name for your document.

4. Click Save.

   Acrobat saves your file in the location you specified.

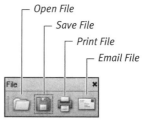

Open File
Save File
Print File
Email File

Figure 3.1 The File toolbar contains tools that let you save or distribute your document.

Figure 3.2 When you select File > Save As, a standard Save As dialog box opens.

SAVING A PDF FILE

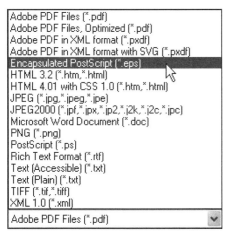

Figure 3.3 The "Save as type" pop-up menu lets you choose from among a large number of file formats to which Acrobat can convert a PDF file.

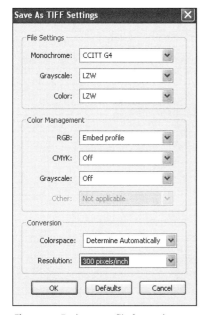

Figure 3.4 Each output file format has a set of controls that dictate the details of the conversion.

Exporting to Other Formats

Acrobat can save a PDF document to a variety of other formats, such as TIFF, PNG, and EPS. This is easily done through the Save As dialog box.

To save a file to a different format:

1. Select File > Save As, or click the Save button on the File toolbar (Figure 3.1)

   In either case, Acrobat will present you with a standard Save-a-File dialog box (Figure 3.2).

2. Choose a file format from the "Save as type" pop-up menu.

   Acrobat offers a large number of file formats to which it can export (**Figure 3.3**).

3. Optionally, click the Settings button, and choose any of the options you need.

   The Settings dialog box opens for the file format you selected (**Figure 3.4**). You can usually use the defaults with no problems. (See the sidebar "TIFF and EPS Options.")

4. Navigate to the folder on your disk in which you want to save your file.

5. Click Save.

   Acrobat saves your document in the file format you specified.

TIFF and EPS Options

Of all the file types to which Acrobat can convert PDF, only two are routinely useful for most people: TIFF and EPS. These are widely used as illustration formats by high-end page layout and graphics software such as Adobe InDesign and Adobe Photoshop.

Most of Acrobat's defaults for these formats' file-type settings are perfectly good. For each of them, however, you should change a couple of these settings. These are *sticky*; once you change them, Acrobat will use the new values until you change them again.

TIFF settings (Figure 3.4):

◆ Change the resolution (at the bottom of the dialog box) to match the device on which the illustration will be printed or displayed:

For a printed document: 300 dpi for laser printers or 1200 dpi for high-resolution printers

For on-screen presentations: 72 dpi

EPS General settings (**Figure 3.5**):

◆ Choose ASCII to ensure compatibility with all networks.

◆ Choose Embedded Fonts to eliminate problems with missing fonts.

◆ Check Convert TrueType to Type 1 to eliminate problems associated with TrueType fonts.

◆ Check Include Preview so that importing applications can more easily work with the file.

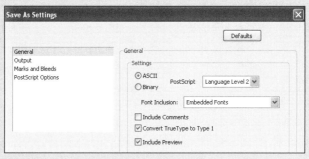

Figure 3.5 The EPS settings shown here always work well.

Export file types

Acrobat can export PDF files to a variety of other file types, listed in the Save As dialog box's "Save file as" pop-up menu (Figure 3.3). Unfortunately, in most cases, the conversion changes the document's appearance: Items move around, fonts change, illustrations come out pixilated, and other problems occur. The conversions work best for simple documents.

That said, there are reasons you may want to save a PDF file to some of these formats. Following is a list of the file types to which Acrobat converts most successfully and the purpose of each.

◆ **Adobe PDF Files** (vector). Acrobat's default file format. Acrobat saves the PDF file as-is.

continues on next page

Vector vs. Bitmap

Each export file type is identified as being either *vector* or *bitmap*.

Vector files retain their quality regardless of the display or printing device. In particular, edges never become jagged, regardless of the zoom level or the printer's resolution (dpi). On the other hand, vector files are prone to missing fonts and images, and other problems that are often hard to diagnose.

Bitmap files consist of a series of full-page images of all the document's pages. This makes them immune to missing fonts and the other problems to which vector formats are prone. However, bitmap files are inherently tied to a device resolution. If the bitmap is intended for a device of one resolution and you print it on a device of another resolution, the results may look bad (**Figure 3.6**).

You should use vector file types unless you have consistent problems with fonts or other hard-to-fix printing problems.

Figure 3.6 Vector file types (left) always look smooth. Bitmap files (right) become jagged if you zoom in on them.

- **Adobe PDF Files, Optimized** (vector). Still a PDF file, but internally reorganized for viewing in a Web browser. Use this type if you'll be posting your PDF file on the Web for people to read online.

- **Encapsulated PostScript** (vector). A file format used for illustrations in high-end graphics and page-layout software. EPS is usually your best choice if the PDF file will be used as an illustration (**Figure 3.7**, top).

- **JPEG** (bitmap). A compact bitmap format widely used for images, including digital photography. It's useful only for photographs; it's particularly bad for general PDF files, because line art and text usually become surrounded by a halo of *artifacts*, as in the bottom text in Figure 3.7.

- **Rich Text Format** (vector). A format that's commonly understood by a wide range of applications, although conversion to it isn't always successful. If you want to convert your PDF file into a word-processing document, this is worth trying.

- **Text (Plain)**. A format that extracts the text in the PDF file, removing all formatting information and illustrations. The text may come out in a scrambled order if it's formatted in multiple columns.

- **Text (Accessible)**. A format that extracts the text from the PDF file and attempts to preserve internal information that makes it easier to use the text with Braille readers. This information must have been put into the PDF file by the creator and is usually absent.

- **TIFF** (bitmap). The best format if you need to convert your PDF pages to a series of images. The format is reasonably compact, and text and line art look much better than in JPEG (Figure 3.7).

Figure 3.7 Here is PDF text exported to (from top to bottom) EPS, TIFF, and JPEG. The JPEG artifacts are somewhat exaggerated, because the text was created with the nondefault "low quality" setting.

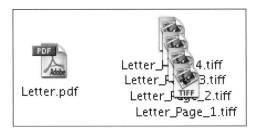

Figure 3.8 When you save a PDF file to a bitmap format, such as JPEG or TIFF, Acrobat creates an image file for each page.

✔ Tips

■ If you need to export your pages to use as illustrations in page-layout or other software, use either EPS or TIFF. EPS is the better choice generally, but if you're having trouble with fonts in the EPS file, go back and resave the PDF file as a TIFF. Keep in mind that because it's a bitmap, the TIFF illustration will become ugly if you scale it. That said, many high-end page layout programs can use PDF files directly as illustrations, without conversion to other formats.

■ If you save a multi-page PDF file in one of the bitmap formats, such as JPEG or TIFF, Acrobat creates one bitmap file per page (**Figure 3.8**).

Minimizing File Size

Once you've saved your document, Acrobat has a feature that looks through the PDF file and makes changes to minimize the size of the file. This process entails rearranging the internal structure of the document and storing repeated graphics in a more efficient form.

You should always do this with PDF files you're going to distribute electronically. It often makes little difference, but sometimes it results in an impressive reduction in file size.

To reduce the size of a PDF file:

1. With your document open, select Document > Reduce File Size.

   The Reduce File Size dialog box opens (**Figure 3.9**).

2. In the pop-up menu, choose the earliest version of Acrobat with which your file must remain compatible (**Figure 3.10**).

   Choosing higher versions of Acrobat may make the resulting file smaller, but it will also prevent people from reading the file if they haven't recently upgraded their version of Acrobat. The default value is "Retain existing"; this means the new file should have the same Acrobat compatibility as the original.

3. Click OK.

   The Save As dialog box opens.

4. Provide a name for the new, slimmed-down file, and click OK.

   Acrobat works for a while and then saves the reduced file with the new name.

Figure 3.9 The Reduce File Size dialog box lets you choose the earliest version of Acrobat with which your file must be compatible.

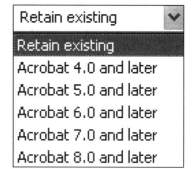

Figure 3.10 Pick the earliest version of Acrobat that your readers may own.

✔ Tips

- You can save the reduced file with the same name as the original if you wish. Doing so erases the original file.

- For optimum trade-off between small file size and broad compatibility, I recommend choosing Acrobat 5 for your compatibility setting. This presumes your file won't be read with an electronic book reader or other device that requires specialized internal information.

Figure 3.11 The Print dialog box lets you choose among a wide range of options. In most cases, the default values work fine.

Printing a Document

Visions of the paperless office notwithstanding, PDF is routinely used to distribute printed documents. After you open a PDF file and peruse it on screen, you may want to print it for reading at your leisure.

To print a PDF document:

1. Choose File > Print, or click the Print tool in the File toolbar.

   Acrobat will present you with the Print dialog box (**Figure 3.11**).

2. Choose the options you want.

   In most cases, you can accept the default values for these controls. Most of them are at least occasionally important, however, and we'll discuss them next.

3. Click OK.

   Acrobat prints your document.

Miscellaneous settings

◆ **Print to file** (Windows). This is a standard Windows check box that tells Acrobat to send the printer code to a file rather than to the printer. This option is used in professional printing to capture PostScript code for the document.

◆ **Print color as black** (Windows). This option converts colors to black. It may be useful if you're printing diagrams with a lot of thin, light-colored lines.

◆ **Printing Tips**. If you're connected to the Internet, clicking this button launches your Web browser and takes you to troubleshooting tips in Adobe's Knowledgebase.

continues on next page

PRINTING A DOCUMENT

✔Tips

■ Don't ignore the preview picture in the Print dialog box (**Figure 3.12**). A quick examination of this picture can tell you whether your document is going to print as you expect.

■ The slider control beneath the preview picture in the Print dialog box lets you step through the pages in your document.

■ Selecting Collate can significantly slow your printing speed, because Acrobat must resend the printing code for each copy of each page in your document. I suggest you routinely leave it off and collate by hand.

■ If the size and position of items on your printed page seem off by a small amount, check to make sure you didn't print the document with Shrink to Fit selected. This option may reduce the size of the page contents by a few percent.

Figure 3.12 The preview picture in the Print dialog box shows you how your printed pages will look. The slider beneath the picture lets you move among the pages.

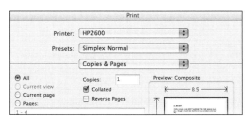

Figure 3.13 The Macintosh Print dialog box has Mac-standard controls at the top, but otherwise it has the same Acrobat-specific controls in Windows.

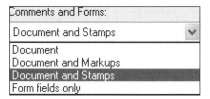

Figure 3.14 The Comments and Forms pop-up menu lets you decide whether to print the contents of annotations and form fields.

Print Options

The Print dialog box (Figure 3.11) presents you with a large collection of choices that determine the details of how your document prints. Although you can usually accept the default values for these options, sometimes you'll need to change some of them.

The Macintosh and Windows versions of this dialog box look superficially different, but the Acrobat-specific controls are entirely identical. The dialog boxes differ only in the controls that are standard to the two environments' Print dialog boxes. For example, at the top of the Macintosh version of this dialog box (**Figure 3.13**) are pop-up menus for Presets and Option categories, whereas Windows has printer status text and a Properties button.

Let's look at the controls and see how they affect your print job. Note that the dialog box's Preview always reflects the controls' current settings:

Printer controls

◆ **Printer Name**. This is the standard pop-up menu of printers available to your computer. Choose the printer on which you want to print.

◆ **Comments and Forms**. This pop-up menu lets you specify whether annotations and form field contents should be printed along with the document pages (**Figure 3.14**).

Print-range controls

◆ **All, Current view, Current page, Pages**.
These four radio buttons choose the pages
within your document that you want to
print. They're self-explanatory, with one
possible exception: The Pages text field
(**Figure 3.15**) can accept a hyphen to
indicate a contiguous range of pages and
commas to separate discontinuous pages.
Thus, 1-4 prints pages 1 through 4, and
1,4,7 prints pages 1, 4, and 7.

◆ **Subset**. This pop-up menu allows you to
choose to print even pages, odd pages, or
both (**Figure 3.16**). It's useful for manually printing duplex documents.

◆ **Reverse pages**. Acrobat prints the pages
in reverse order. This is convenient if your
printer delivers its pages face-up; the
stack of output ends up in correct order.

Page-handling controls

◆ **Copies**. Specify the number of copies you
want of each page.

◆ **Collate**. If you print multiple copies of
a document, the pages are collated.

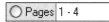

Figure 3.15 The Pages text field accepts hyphens to
indicate a contiguous range of pages and commas
to separate, individual pages.

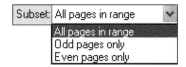

Figure 3.16 The Subset pop-up menu
allows you to print even, odd, or
all pages.

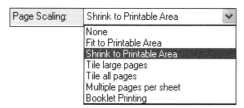

Figure 3.17 The Page Scaling menu tells Acrobat to scale the document pages at print time in a variety of useful ways.

Figure 3.18 Fit to Printable Area scales the page up or down until it exactly fits within the current paper.

Figure 3.19 Auto-Rotate and Center moves the contents of the document page so they're centered on the paper.

◆ **Page Scaling**. This menu lets you resize the document pages in a variety of ways (**Figure 3.17**). The most routinely useful selections are as follows:

▲ None prints the document in its native size; this is usually what you want.

▲ Shrink to Printable Area shrinks the page so it fits within the printer's native printable area. This ensures items near the edges of your pages (such as headers and footers) print successfully.

▲ Fit to Printable Area shrinks or expands the page so it fits within the printer's native printable area. This makes the document page as large as it can be without losing information off the edges of the paper (**Figure 3.18**).

We'll look at other selections in this menu later in this chapter.

◆ **Auto-Rotate and Center**. This option repositions the page so it's centered on the paper (**Figure 3.19**). It may also rotate the page if Acrobat thinks it's necessary (usually not). This may be useful if you want to center a small document page on a large piece of paper.

◆ **Choose Paper Source by PDF page size** (Windows). This option overrides the printer's default paper size and uses each page's paper size as specified in the PDF file. It's useful if you have a document whose pages vary in size and a printer with multiple paper trays; Acrobat selects paper from whichever tray most closely matches the page's size.

PRINT OPTIONS

Printing Multiple Pages per Sheet

You'll commonly want to be able to print two or more pages of your document on each piece of paper. Acrobat's Print dialog box lets you do this easily.

To print multiple pages on each printed page:

1. Select File > Print.

   The Print dialog box opens.

2. In the Page Scaling pop-up menu, choose "Multiple pages per sheet".

   Acrobat displays additional controls beneath the Page Scaling pop-up menu (**Figure 3.20**). In addition, the Print dialog box's Preview reflects the multiple pages (**Figure 3.21**).

3. In the "Pages per sheet" pop-up menu, choose the number of pages you want on each sheet of paper.

   As always, the Preview picture shows the change.

4. Click OK.

   Acrobat prints your document with the specified number of pages on each sheet of paper.

✔ Tips

- If you choose Custom from the "Pages per sheet" pop-up menu, you can specify how many pages you want across and down each sheet (**Figure 3.22**).

- I often make a reference page with thumbnails of all of my document's pages by printing with 16 pages per sheet. The text is unreadable, but it provides me with a usable overview of my document's layout.

Figure 3.20 When you choose "Multiple pages per sheet" from the Page Scaling menu, Acrobat displays additional controls.

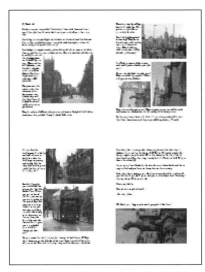

Figure 3.21 The Preview picture in the Print dialog box reflects the number of pages you're printing on each sheet of paper.

Figure 3.22 If you choose Custom from the "Pages per sheet" menu, you can specify how many pages you want across and down each sheet.

Figure 3.23 To turn a four-page document into a booklet, Acrobat prints pages 4 and 1 on one side of the paper and pages 2 and 3 on the other.

Figure 3.24 Fold the paper to make your booklet. For longer documents, stack the paper, and staple the stack in the middle before folding.

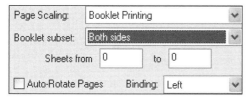

Figure 3.25 When you choose Booklet Printing, Acrobat displays additional controls that let you specify the details.

Printing a Booklet

Sometimes, when proofing a document, it's useful to turn a PDF file into a booklet. When you choose this feature, Acrobat prints your document two pages per sheet of paper, double-sided, reordering the pages as needed to make a booklet (**Figures 3.23** and **3.24**).

To print a document as a booklet:

1. Select File > Print.

    Acrobat will display the Print dialog box .

2. In the Page Scaling pop-up menu, choose Booklet Printing.

    Acrobat displays additional controls beneath the Page Scaling pop-up menu (**Figure 3.25**). As always, the Preview reflects the new arrangement of the pages.

continues on next page

PRINTING A BOOKLET

3. In the "Booklet subset" pop-up menu, choose "Front side only" or "Back side only" (**Figure 3.26**) if you want to print only one side of each sheet of paper.

   These options let you print a booklet on a printer that can't print double-sided. You can print the front sides of all the pages, put the paper back into the printer, and then print the back sides.

4. In the "Sheets from…to" fields, type the beginning and end of the range of paper sheets you want to print.

   Confusingly, putting a zero in both of these fields means "print all the sheets." This is what you'll usually want.

5. In the Binding pop-up menu, specify whether the booklet will be bound on the left or the right.

6. Click OK.

   Acrobat prints your document as a booklet.

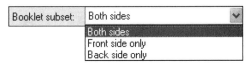

Figure 3.26 Printing the front and back sides separately allows you to print a booklet on a printer that doesn't print double-sided.

Printing Terminology

Here are some terms you may encounter when reading about printing:

◆ **Duplex**. Printing on both sides of a sheet of paper.

◆ **Simplex**. Printing on only one side of each sheet of paper.

◆ **2-up, 3-up, and so on.** Printing more than one page on each sheet. The number is the number of pages per sheet.

◆ **Imposition.** Rearranging pages for printing a book. The verb is "to impose."

Using these terms, you can say that to make a booklet, your document is printed 2-up, duplex, imposed.

MAKING PDF FILES

PDF is arguably the best file format for storage and distribution of documents. It's compact, it supports a wide variety of content (including text, images, line art, and multimedia), and it's freely usable without licensing fees. However, all this capability is useless unless you can conveniently make PDF files. This is the topic we address in this chapter.

When you install Acrobat, you also install features into your computer system that make it easy and quick to generate PDF files from within virtually any Macintosh or Windows application. Furthermore, Acrobat has many powerful features that let you create PDF files: You can convert many common file types to PDF, scan paper documents directly into PDF, convert Web pages to PDF files, and combine several PDF files into a single document.

In this chapter, you'll learn how to do all of these.

Printing to a PDF File

Acrobat makes it easy to create PDF files from within any application. When you install Acrobat, you also install onto your computer system a virtual printer called Adobe PDF (**Figure 4.1**). When you print to this printer, it converts the document being printed into a PDF file rather than producing sheets of paper.

The nice thing about this feature is that it works with any Macintosh or Windows application that prints.

To print to a PDF file:

1. Choose File > Print from within your application.

   Your system's standard Print dialog box opens (**Figure 4.2**).

2. In the Printer pop-up menu, choose Adobe PDF 8.0.

3. Click Print.

   A standard Save dialog box opens.

4. Type a name for your PDF file.

5. Click OK.

   After a short while, you will see a newly created PDF file on your disk.

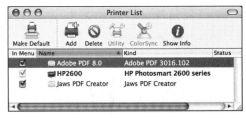

Figure 4.1 Acrobat installs onto your system a virtual printer named Adobe PDF 8.0. When printed to, this printer creates a PDF file.

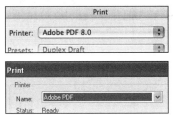

Figure 4.2 You use the Adobe PDF printer by choosing it as the current printer in the standard Print dialog box.

Adobe PDF Options

Adobe PDF defines a set of options, available through the Print dialog box, that affect the PDF it produces. Although Acrobat's default values for these options are the most sensible choices in most cases, you may want to look them over.

You access the PDF options from the standard Print dialog box by clicking the Properties button in Windows or, on the Mac, by choosing PDF Options in the pop-up menu just below the Presets menu (**Figure 4.3**).

See the Acrobat Help files for the meanings of each of these controls.

Figure 4.3 Some print options affect Adobe PDF's behavior. The default values work well.

Figure 4.4 Acrobat 8 installs a Make PDF toolbar in Microsoft Office. The two tools are Convert to PDF and Convert to PDF and Email.

Figure 4.5 As PDF Maker creates its PDF file, it displays a progress bar.

Using PDFMaker in Microsoft Office

Acrobat 8 automatically installs a PDFMaker toolbar into the Microsoft Office suite of software (**Figure 4.4**).

This toolbar includes two tools: one that creates a PDF file out of the current document, and another that emails the current document as a PDF file to an address of your choice.

To create a PDF file in an Office application:

1. With your Office document active, make the PDF Maker toolbar visible, if necessary, by choosing View > Toolbars > Adobe Acrobat PDF Maker 8.

2. Click the Convert to Adobe PDF button. Office will present you with the standard Save-a-File dialog box.

3. Specify a name and location for your PDF file.

4. Click OK. Acrobat creates the PDF file, displaying a progress bar (**Figure 4.5**) while it works.

✔ Tip

■ PDFMaker uses the Adobe PDF virtual printer behind the scenes, so don't be alarmed if your Office application seems to be printing in the background when you use this toolbar.

To email an Office document as PDF:

1. With your Office document open, click the Convert to Adobe PDF and Email button. The standard Save dialog box opens.

2. Specify a name and location for your PDF file.

3. Click OK.

   Acrobat creates the PDF file, displaying a progress bar (Figure 4.5) while it works.

   When it's finished, PDFMaker launches your email client software and opens a blank email window with the new PDF file already attached (**Figure 4.6**).

4. Fill out the destination address and subject in your email client.

5. Click your email client's Send button.

✔ Tip

■ In Windows, depending on your email client, PDFMaker may ask you for an email address and subject and send the PDF file directly, without launching your email client.

Figure 4.6 The Convert to PDF and Email tool launches your mail client and opens a blank message that has the new PDF file attached to it.

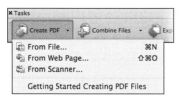

Figure 4.7 The Create PDF menu in the Tasks toolbar lets you create a PDF file from a variety of sources.

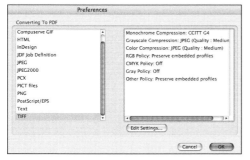

Figure 4.8 Acrobat's Preferences let you specify the details of how it converts the various file formats to PDF.

Converting Images and Other Files to PDF

Acrobat can convert a variety of file types to PDF and then open them in a document window. The list of supported file types includes all the common vector and image formats (see the sidebar "Conversion File Types").

Converting these files to PDF is remarkably easy.

To convert a file to PDF:

1. In Acrobat, choose File > Create PDF > From File; or, in the Tasks toolbar, choose Create PDF > From File (**Figure 4.7**).

   Acrobat will present you with a standard Pick-a-File dialog box.

2. Choose the file that you want to convert to PDF.

   Acrobat converts the file to PDF and opens it in a new document window.

3. If you want to save the document on your disk, choose File > Save As.

✔ Tip

- Acrobat's Preferences include a large collection of controls that determine how it converts files to PDF. The default values for these controls are sensible and should generally be left alone. However, as you gain experience, you may find it interesting to look at them. Go to Acrobat > Preferences on the Mac or Edit > Preferences in Windows to get to the Convert To PDF options (**Figure 4.8**).

Conversion File Types

Acrobat can convert the following types of files to PDF:

- BMP
- Compuserve GIF
- HTML
- InDesign
- JPEG
- JPEG2000

- PCX
- PICT
- PNG
- PostScript/EPS
- Text
- TIFF

This list encompasses all the most common graphic, design, and image formats.

CONVERTING IMAGE AND OTHER FILES TO PDF

Scanning Directly to PDF

Acrobat can use your scanner to scan directly to a PDF document. Acrobat can operate any scanner with a TWAIN or (in Windows XP) WIA driver. Most scanners install on a computer with one or both of these drivers.

Figure 4.9 The Tasks toolbar lets you scan a paper document directly to PDF.

Remember that if you scan a text document, the result is a *picture* of the text, not the text itself; the resulting document isn't searchable. Acrobat can use Optical Character Recognition (OCR) technology to convert the scanned text to real text; you'll see how to do this in Chapter 16.

To scan a page directly to PDF:

1. Choose File > Create PDF > From Scanner; or, on the Tasks toolbar, choose Create PDF > From Scanner (**Figure 4.9**).

   The Acrobat Scan dialog box opens (**Figure 4.10**).

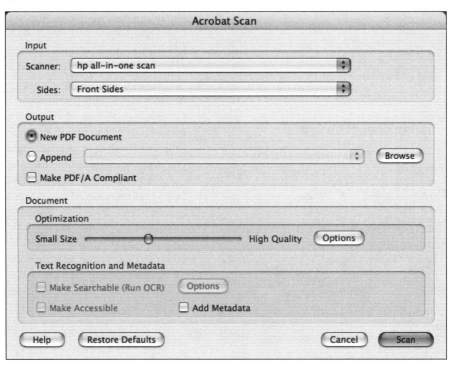

Figure 4.10 The Acrobat Scan dialog box lets you control how your scanned document is converted to PDF.

SCANNING DIECTLY TO PDF

2. From the Scanner pop-up menu, choose the scanner you want to use.

This menu lists all the TWAIN and WIA scanners visible to your computer.

3. Choose the settings for the scan:

▲ If your scanner can do double-sided scans, choose Front Sides or Both Sides from the Sides pop-up menu.

▲ If you want to convert scanned text to searchable text, choose the Make Searchable check box.

The remaining controls in this dialog box are best left at their default settings. Check Acrobat Help for a description of these controls.

5. Click Scan.

Acrobat scans your document and opens the result in a new PDF document window.

6. Choose File > Save As to save your new PDF file on your disk.

✔ Tip

■ You can choose the Append radio button in the Acrobat Scan dialog box to add your scanned page to the end of an existing PDF file.

SCANNING DIECTLY TO PDF

Merging PDF Files

Acrobat can combine multiple files into a single PDF file. The component files may be PDF files, TIFFs, EPS files, or files of any format that Acrobat can convert to PDF. This is extremely useful for combining, say, all the files associated with an invoice—the invoice itself, an expense report, scanned receipts—into a single emailable file.

To merge several PDF files into a single PDF file:

1. Choose File > Combine Files; or, on the Tasks toolbar, choose Combine Files > Merge Files (**Figure 4.11**).

   The Combine Files dialog box opens (**Figure 4.12**). This dialog box lets you choose a list of files to combine.

2. Choose from the available options:
   - ▲ **Add Files** allows you to add individual files to the list.
   - ▲ **Add Folders** lets you choose a folder, all of whose convertible contents will be added to the list.
   - ▲ **Reuse Files** lets you choose files inside a PDF package. (We'll talk about PDF packages in the next section.)
   - ▲ **Add Open Files** allows you to choose among the files currently open in Acrobat.

   No matter which option you choose, an Open dialog box appropriate to the task opens (**Figure 4.13**).

   The list of files currently selected is displayed in the Combine multiple files dialog box. You can click the Move Up and Move Down arrows beneath the list to alter the files' order.

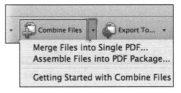

Figure 4.11 The Merge Files menu on the Tasks toolbar lets you combine several files into a single PDF file.

Figure 4.12 This dialog box lets you choose the files you want to merge together.

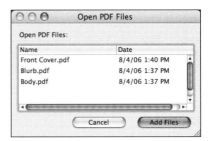

Figure 4.13 Each of the Add options present you with an Open dialog box appropriate to the type of files.

Figure 4.14 Having selected your list of files, you now tell Acrobat into what kind of file you want to combine them.

Figure 4.15 After it merges your files, Acrobat lets you see an overview of the new, combined PDF file.

3. When your list of files is complete, click Next.

The Combine multiple files dialog box displays a pair of radio buttons that let you specify the kind of file into which to save your files (**Figure 4.14**).

4. Choose the Merge files into a Single PDF button.

5. Click Create.

Acrobat merges the files together and opens the Combine Files Complete dialog box (**Figure 4.15**).

6. Click the Save button.

Acrobat asks you for a name and location for your merged file and then saves the new PDF file onto your hard disk.

✔ Tips

■ In Figure 4.12, you see three radio buttons running along the bottom of the dialog box; they let you choose a qualitative file size (smaller, default, or larger). These options mostly affect how images are stored in your PDF file. The smaller the file, the less image information Acrobat retains in the merged file. As a corollary, if there are no images in your PDF files, you will probably see little difference among these options.

■ Acrobat creates bookmarks in the merged file that take you to the start of each of the original documents. (See Chapter 2 for a reminder of how to use bookmarks.)

MERGING PDF FILES

Creating a PDF Package

PDF packages are new to Acrobat 8. When you combine PDF files into a new PDF file, the original files cease to exist; they become pages in the new file. If you combine PDF files into a PDF package, however, the original files retain their identities. Each file can have its own password protection, its own set of electronic signatures, and its own form fields that don't conflict with fields elsewhere in the package. This allows all the documents associated with, say, a patient's medical file—including consent forms, scanned lab results, and doctor recommendations—to be bundled into a single "wrapper" without losing the individual files' characteristics.

If you open a PDF package in Acrobat 8, the left side of the resulting document window displays a list of the individual files that make up the package (**Figure 4.16**). Clicking a file name in the list takes you to that component file within the package.

The first several steps in creating a package are identical to those for merging files into a single PDF file.

To merge several PDF files into a PDF package:

1. Follow steps 1–3 of the task "To merge several PDF files into a single PDF file."

2. In the Combine multiple files dialog box, choose the "Assemble files into a PDF Package" radio button.

3. Click the Create button.

   Acrobat creates the new package and opens the Combine Files Complete dialog box (**Figure 4.17**).

4. Click the Save button.

   Acrobat asks you for a name and location and then saves the new package file onto your hard disk.

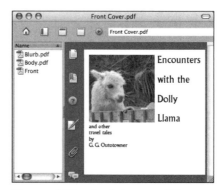

Figure 4.16 When Acrobat opens a PDF package, the document window lists the component files.

Figure 4.17 When it finishes creating the package, Acrobat presents you with a report that lets you preview the package.

Package Cover Sheets

Packages are new to Acrobat 8 and aren't readable by earlier versions of Acrobat. If a reader opens a package in an earlier version of Acrobat, they see the package's *cover sheet.*

The default cover sheet is a page that tells the reader that this PDF file is actually a package and directs them to get the latest Adobe Reader (**Figure 4.18**).

However, the Combine multiple files dialog box lets you alternatively specify that the first document in the package should be used as the cover sheet. In this case, users who open the package in an earlier version of Acrobat see only the first document; the rest of the package's contents are hidden.

To use the package's first document as the cover sheet, choose the Use first document radio button in the lower-right section of the Combine Multiple Files dialog box (**Figure 4.19**).

Figure 4.18 The default cover sheet for a package urges the reader to get the current version of Adobe Reader.

Figure 4.19 If you wish, a package can use the first component document as its cover sheet.

Converting Web Pages to PDF

Acrobat can convert a Web page or an entire Web site into a single PDF file. The result is a self-contained PDF version of the original Web page, with all images and graphics intact and with functioning links.

I use this feature to convert online manuals and other documentation into a PDF file that I can keep, read, and search offline.

To convert a Web site to PDF:

1. Choose File > Create PDF > From Web Page; or, on the Tasks toolbar, choose Create PDF > From Web Page (**Figure 4.20**).

   Acrobat will present you with the Create PDF From Web Page dialog box (**Figure 4.21**).

2. In the URL field, type the complete Web address of the Web page you want to convert to PDF.

3. Choose settings for the conversion:
   - ▲ In the "Get only" field, type the depth to which you want to convert the site. (See the sidebar "Web Site Conversion Settings.")
   - ▲ Choose both "Stay on same path" and "Stay on same server."

Figure 4.20 The Tasks toolbar lets you create a PDF file from a Web page or an entire Web site.

Figure 4.21 The Create PDF from Web Page dialog box has important controls that limit the scope of your Web conversion.

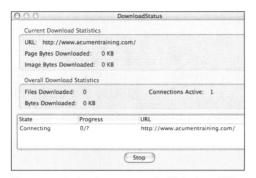

Figure 4.22 As Acrobat converts the Web site to PDF, it displays its progress.

4. Click Create.

Acrobat displays the Download Status dialog box (**Figure 4.22**), showing you how the conversion is progressing.

When the conversion is finished, Acrobat displays the converted Web page or site in a document window. Note that there will be some differences in the text and graphics when they are converted. These changes are usually comparable to how a page's appearance changes from one Web browser to another.

Web Site Conversion Settings

The controls in the Create PDF from Web Page dialog box (Figure 4.21) have the critical purpose of limiting the scope of your Web capture. They keep you from, at one extreme, inadvertently trying to convert the entire World Wide Web into a single (large!) PDF file:

◆ **Get only *n* level(s).** Here you specify the extent to which Acrobat should grab Web pages that are the target of links on your selected Web page. A value of 1 says to get only the Web page whose address you have specified. A value of 2 says to get that Web page and any pages linked to by that page. A value of 3 additionally captures pages linked to by *those* pages, and so forth.

Keep this number small. The larger the number of levels you specify, the exponentially longer the conversion will take.

◆ **Get entire site.** As it says, this option converts the entire site to PDF. I recommend against this approach unless you're certain the Web site isn't too extensive.

◆ **Stay on same path.** Like all files, the HTML files that make up a Web site reside in a directory on a hard disk—in this case, the Web server's disk. This option prevents Acrobat from following links that reside outside of the target Web page's location or its subdirectories. I recommend choosing this.

◆ **Stay on the same server.** Acrobat won't follow links off your target page's server. I strongly recommend this option. Otherwise, for example, if the page you request has links to its sponsors, you may find yourself trying to convert all of Microsoft's Web site to a PDF file.

CONVERTING WEB PAGES TO PDF

Converting Screen Shots to PDF

This is a Macintosh-only feature. When it's selected, Acrobat lets you capture the contents of a window, a region, or the entire screen to a PDF file. This is convenient for people who write computer documentation.

To capture the entire screen to PDF:

1. Choose File > Create PDF > From Screen Capture (**Figure 4.23**).

   After a moment, Acrobat will present you with a document window containing an image of the entire screen.

2. Choose File > Save As to save this file to disk.

To capture a window to PDF:

1. Choose File > Create PDF > From Window Capture.

   The mouse pointer changes to a camera. As the pointer moves over the windows open on the screen, the current window turns blue.

2. Click the window whose contents you want to capture.

   A document opens, containing an image of the window you clicked.

3. Choose File > Save As to save this file to disk.

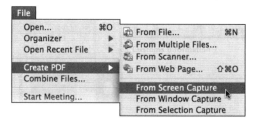

Figure 4.23 On the Macintosh, Acrobat can capture parts of your computer screen and convert the image to PDF.

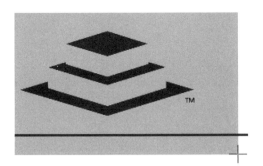

Figure 4.24 When capturing a part of the screen, you drag out a light-gray rectangle that indicates the capture area.

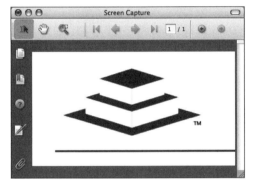

Figure 4.25 The area of the screen you selected is turned into a PDF image.

To capture a region of the desktop to PDF:

1. Choose File > Create PDF > From Screen Capture (Figure 4.23).

   The mouse pointer changes to a crosshair.

2. Click and drag a rectangular marquee around the area you want to capture.

   Acrobat uses a nonstandard marquee with this tool: You drag out a light-gray area on the screen (**Figure 4.24**).

   Acrobat will present you with a document containing the contents of the region you enclosed (**Figure 4.25**).

3. Choose File > Save As to save this file to disk.

CONVERTING SCEEN SHOTS TO PDF

ADDING COMMENTS TO A DOCUMENT

5

One of the longest-standing features in Acrobat is the ability to add comments to a PDF document. Originally, these comments were simple, electronic sticky notes that a reader could attach to the page. The PDF annotation mechanism has since grown to include a broad set of highlighting, drawing, and other tools that you can use to do fully featured commentary on a document. Additionally, there are tools for reading and summarizing these comments, and even for conducting a document review involving your entire workgroup or company.

The annotation feature in Acrobat is so extensive and important that it will occupy three chapters in this book, concentrating on adding comments to a document, reading and managing those documents, and conducting an enterprise-wide review of a document.

Examining Acrobat's Commenting Tools

Acrobat's commenting tools are accessible in three locations:

◆ The Comments > Comment & Markup Tools submenu (**Figure 5.1**) contains icons for all the comment tools.

◆ The Tasks toolbar has a drop-down menu containing all the comment tools (**Figure 5.2**).

◆ The Comment & Markup toolbar includes tools for the most commonly used comment tools (**Figure 5.3**).

You may add buttons to the Comment & Markup toolbar for the missing tools; Chapter 1 provides directions for adding tools to a toolbar.

Figure 5.1 All the comment tools are available through the Comments menu.

Figure 5.2 The tools are also available through the Tasks toolbar.

Figure 5.3 The most commonly used comment tools are on the Comment & Markup toolbar.

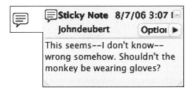

Figure 5.4 Every comment has an icon that represents its position on the page.

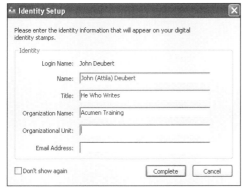

Figure 5.5 Most comments also have a pop-up window that holds the text for that comment.

![Identity Setup dialog box]

Figure 5.6 When you first use the comment tools, Acrobat may ask you for some information about yourself. This is strictly optional.

Comment icons and pop-ups

Every comment on a page has two visual parts.

The comment's *icon* is a graphic that indicates the position of the comment on the page (**Figure 5.4**). This is different for each comment type: a speech bubble for Sticky Notes, a piece of text for a Text Box, and a "sign here" pointer for a Stamp.

Most comments also have a *pop-up window* that displays the text associated with the comment (**Figure 5.5**). Double-clicking the comment's icon opens its pop-up, allowing you to read and edit the comment's text.

✔ Tips

- Acrobat's Preferences dialog box has a pane full of controls determining the behavior of comments. The default values for these options are sensible, so you can safely ignore them. However, once you've worked with comments for a while, you may want take a look at them. Choose Edit > Preferences to see Acrobat's preferences.

- The first time you use one of Acrobat's comment tools, it may present you with a dialog box that asks for your name, company, and other information (**Figure 5.6**). Acrobat uses this information for some of its dynamic comments that add your name and other data to the comment on the fly.

Adding a Sticky Note to a Page

The Sticky Note comment is Acrobat's oldest annotation type, dating back to Acrobat 1.0. This annotation type is the functional equivalent of the paper sticky note after which it's named; it holds a small amount of text attached to the page in a pop-up window.

To add a sticky note to a page:

1. Click the Sticky Note tool in the Comment & Markup toolbar.

   The mouse pointer turns into crosshairs.

2. Click the page.

   Acrobat places the comment's icon on the page and opens the comment's pop-up window (**Figure 5.7**).

3. Type the text you want for the comment into the pop-up window.

✔ Tips

- To change the location of a comment's icon, click it and then drag it to a new location.

- You can change the text of an existing comment. To do so, double-click the icon to get to the pop-up, and then click the text and edit it as usual. This works with any type of comment that has text.

Figure 5.7 When you place a Sticky Note on the page, Acrobat opens a pop-up window into which you can type your text.

Figure 5.8 Sticky Notes may be represented on the page by a variety of icons.

Figure 5.9 You change a Sticky Note's icon (and other characteristics) by modifying its properties.

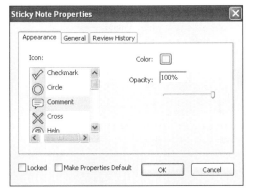

Figure 5.10 The Sticky Note Properties dialog box lets you modify a variety of appearance settings.

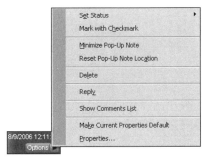

Figure 5.11 You can also get to a comment's properties by clicking the pop-up window's Options control.

A Sticky Note's default icon is a speech bubble. This is a perfectly serviceable icon, but Acrobat supplies a collection of other icons that may be used with Sticky Notes (**Figure 5.8**).

To change a Sticky Note's icon:

1. Right-click the comment's icon to get a contextual menu.

2. Select Properties in the contextual menu (**Figure 5.9**).

   Acrobat will present you with the Sticky Note Properties dialog box (**Figure 5.10**).

3. Choose a new icon from the list.

4. If you want this icon to become the default icon for future Sticky Note comments, click the Make Properties Default check box.

5. To change the note's color, click the Color button and choose a new color from the resulting color picker.

6. To change the opacity of the note, drag the Opacity slider to the desired level.

7. Click OK.

✔ Tips

■ You can prevent a comment from being edited by clicking the Locked check box shown in Figure 5.10.

■ You can delete a comment the way you delete most everything else in the computer world: Select it with your mouse, and then press the Delete key. If you're a Macintosh user, you need to either use the Forward Delete key or hold down the function (Fn) key and press the normal (backspace) Delete key.

■ You can also get to the contextual menu by clicking the little Options arrow in a comment's pop-up window (**Figure 5.11**).

Adding a Text Box Comment

Text Box comments are similar to Sticky Notes, but they have no pop-up window. Instead, the comment displays its text in a rectangular, editable field directly on the page (**Figure 5.12**).

To place a Text Box comment on the page:

1. Click the Text Box tool in the Comment & Markup toolbar.

2. Click and drag a rectangle on the page.
   Acrobat places the Text Box at that location on the page.

3. Type your comment into the text box.

Having placed your Text Box on the page, you can move it around and resize it very easily.

To move and resize a Text Box:

1. Select the Hand or Selection tool, if necessary. These are located in the Select & Zoom toolbar (**Figure 5.13**).

2. Click the Text Box.
   Handles appear at the sides and corners of the Text Box (**Figure 5.14**).

3. Click and drag the Text Box to change its position on the page.

4. Click and drag one of the handles to change the box's size.

Figure 5.12 A Text Box comment presents a text annotation in a rectangular field placed directly on the page.

Figure 5.13 The Select & Zoom toolbar has the Selection tool and the Hand tool, both of which may be used to move a comment's icon around on the page.

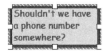

Figure 5.14 When you select a comment's icon, handles appear at the corners and sides.

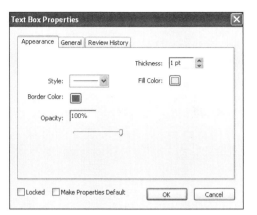

Figure 5.15 The Text Box Properties dialog box lets you change the appearance of the box that contains the text.

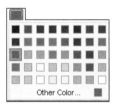

Figure 5.16 Clicking one of the color-well controls results in a standard color picker.

You can also control a Text Box's appearance to quite a large extent. Following are instructions for changing some of these characteristics.

To change a Text Box's colors:

1. With the Hand or Selection tool selected, right-click the Text Box to get a contextual menu.

2. Select Properties at the bottom of the contextual menu.

   Acrobat will present you with the Text Box Properties dialog box (**Figure 5.15**).

3. Click the square color-well control for the border color.

   The color well drops down a standard color picker (**Figure 5.16**).

4. Choose the color you want for your border.

5. Repeat steps 3 and 4 for the fill color.

6. Click OK.

✔ Tip

- If you examine the Text Box Properties dialog box, you'll see that you can also change the style and thickness of the Text Box's border and the box's opacity. Feel free to experiment with these settings.

Finally, you can change the font and other characteristics of the text inside the Text Box. This take a bit more effort, because it requires the Properties toolbar (**Figure 5.17**).

To change a Text Box's font and text size:

1. Make the Properties bar visible, if necessary; to do so, choose View > Toolbars > Properties Bar.

continues on next page

Figure 5.17 The Properties bar presents information on whatever is selected on the page. You can use it to change the characteristics of text.

ADDING A TEXT BOX COMMENT

2. Select the Hand or Selection tool in the Select & Zoom toolbar.
3. Double-click the text in the Text Box.
   A blinking cursor appears at the point where you double-clicked.
4. Choose the text in the Text Box whose font or size you want to change.
   The Properties bar reports the current font and size.
5. In the Properties bar, change the font and size to the values you want.
6. Click outside the Text Box to finish.

✔ Tips

- The Properties bar allows you to change many characteristic of your text, including alignment, color, and placement above or below the baseline (**Figure 5.18**).
- You can also change the style of your text to some combination of bold and italic. Once you've selected text in the Text Box (step 4 in the previous task), right-click the text, and select Text Style in the contextual menu (**Figure 5.19**).

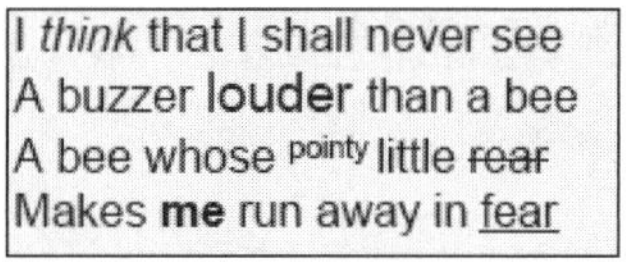
I think that I shall never see
A buzzer louder than a bee
A bee whose pointy little fear
Makes me run away in fear

Figure 5.18 Using the Properties bar, you can change the font, size, and style of your text.

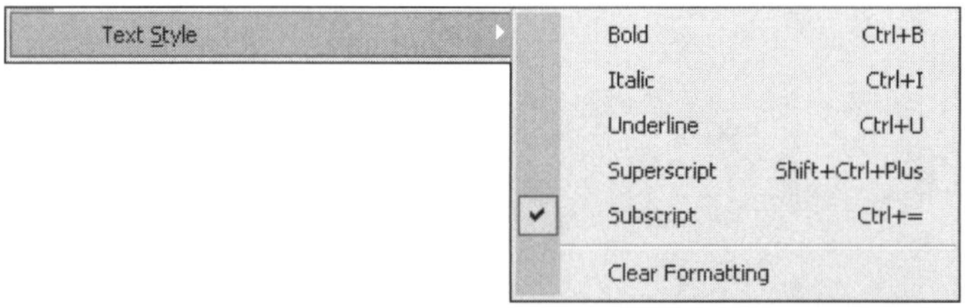
Text Style
Bold Ctrl+B
Italic Ctrl+I
Underline Ctrl+U
Superscript Shift+Ctrl+Plus
Subscript Ctrl+=
Clear Formatting

Figure 5.19 You can change the style of your text with the Text Style submenu.

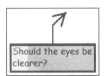

Figure 5.20 A Callout comment is just a Text Box with an arrow.

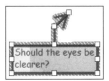

Figure 5.21 Clicking a Callout gives you handles you can use to position the arrow.

Adding a Callout Comment

Callout comments are Text Boxes with an arrow attached (**Figure 5.20**). They allow you to point to the object on the page that your comment discusses.

To add a Callout comment to a page:

1. In the Comment & Markup toolbar, select the Callout tool.

2. Click and drag a rectangle on the page. Acrobat adds a Callout comment with a default arrow pointing at nothing in particular.

3. Type your comment into the text field.

4. Click the border of the comment to make handles appear (**Figure 5.21**).

5. Drag the handles to position the arrow as you want it.

Callout comments have the same set of properties as Text Boxes (font, point size, etc.). See the previous section for a discussion of these properties and instructions on how to change them.

ADDING A CALLOUT COMMENT

Adding Lines and Arrows

Several of Acrobat's commenting tools allow you to add graphic items to your document's pages. The Line and Arrow tools let you add lines and arrows to the page (**Figure 5.22**).

To add a line or an arrow to the page:

1. Click the Line or Arrow tool in the Comment & Markup toolbar.

2. Click and hold on the page at one end of your line or arrow.

3. While holding the mouse button, drag to where you want the other end of the line or arrow to go.

4. Release the mouse button.

✔ Tips

- Lines can be turned into arrows and vice versa. In the Properties dialog box (right-click the item and select Properties in the resulting contextual menu), you can apply an End type to the line (**Figure 5.23**). A value of None turns an arrow into a line; a value of Open (for *open arrow*) turns a line into an arrow. Notice in the figure that several other line ends are available.

- You can reverse an arrow by right-clicking it and selecting Flip Arrow in the contextual menu.

- Like most comments, lines and arrows can have text associated with them. Double-click the line or arrow to see its pop-up window. Even when the pop-up window is closed, you can tell that an arrow or line (or any graphic annotation) has a text comment because Acrobat adds a tiny speech bubble to it (**Figure 5.24**).

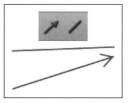

Figure 5.22 The Arrow and Line tools let you draw arrows and lines on the page. This explains their names.

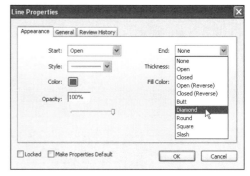

Figure 5.23 The Line Properties dialog box lets you add an End to a line, converting it into an arrow. Selecting None turns an arrow into a line.

Figure 5.24 A comment icon that has text associated with it displays a tiny speech bubble.

Figure 5.25 The Oval tool can be used to circle items of interest on the page.

Figure 5.26 The Rectangle and Oval tools have icons on the Comment & Markup toolbar.

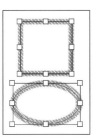

Figure 5.27 Clicking a Rectangle or an Oval icon produces handles you can use to resize that icon.

Drawing Ovals and Rectangles

The Oval and Rectangle comment tools allow you to call attention to items on the Acrobat page (**Figure 5.25**). These tools are available on the Comment & Markup toolbar or from the Comments > Comment & Markup submenu.

To add an Oval or Rectangle comment to the page:

1. Click the Rectangle or the Oval tool in the Comment & Markup toolbar (**Figure 5.26**).

    The mouse pointer changes to crosshairs.

2. Click and hold the mouse on the page.

3. While holding down the mouse button, drag the mouse.

    Acrobat draws a Rectangle or Oval that follows as you drag the mouse.

4. Release the mouse.

    Acrobat adds the Oval or Rectangle to the page.

5. Click the Oval or Rectangle.

    Acrobat adds handles to the sides and corners (**Figure 5.27**).

6. Reposition and resize the graphic as you wish.

✔ Tip

■ You can get a perfect square or circle by holding down the Option/Alt key while dragging the mouse in step 3.

Adding Polygons and Clouds

The polygon-related comment tools work the way similar tools work in most graphics software: You click sequentially on the vertices of the shape you want, and Acrobat connects the dots, making the polygon.

Acrobat supplies three different polygon annotation tools (**Figure 5.28**), only one of which resides in the Comment & Markup toolbar:

◆ **Polygon tool.** This tool creates a closed polygon. When you're finished clicking vertices, Acrobat adds a final side that connects the last point with the first.

◆ **Polygon Line tool.** This is identical to the Polygon tool, except that Acrobat doesn't close the figure for you.

◆ **Cloud tool.** This is identical to the Polygon tool, except that Acrobat draws the polygon as a cloud, as in Figure 5.28.

Unfortunately, only the Cloud tool is available in the Comment & Markup toolbar; you can add the others following the steps in Chapter 1.

Figure 5.28 There are three polygon-related comment tools Polygon: Polygon Line, and Cloud.

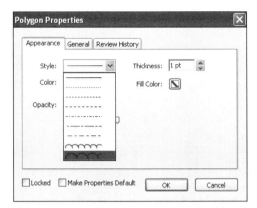

Figure 5.29 You can turn a polygon into a cloud by changing its line style.

To add a Polygon or Cloud to a page:

1. Do one of the following:

▲ To add a cloud, click the Cloud tool in the Comment & Markup toolbar.

▲ To add a closed polygon, select Tools > Comment & Markup > Polygon Tool.

▲ To add an open polygon, select Tools > Comment & Markup > Polygon Line Tool.

2. Click the starting point of your polygon or cloud.

3. Click sequentially on all the corners in your polygon.

Acrobat draws the line segments as you go so you can see how your polygon or cloud is looking.

4. Double-click the final point to finish the polygon.

✔ Tip

■ You can convert polygons to clouds and vice versa. Right-click the object, and look at its properties. One of the controls is a pop-up menu of line styles (**Figure 5.29**). Choose one of the cloud styles to convert your polygon to a cloud.

Text Edits

Acrobat provides a complete set of tools for indicating changes that need to be made to text on a page. These include annotations to mark text for replacement and deletion and to mark an insertion point for missing text.

The way in which you mark up text is a little counterintuitive at first, but it quickly becomes second nature with practice. Broadly, there are two steps to indicating a text change:

1. Indicate the position of the change.

   This entails placing the cursor at the location of an insertion or selecting the text that needs to be deleted or changed.

2. Apply the comment for the markup you want.

The tools you use to do this are most conveniently accessed through the Text Edits menu on the Comment & Markup toolbar (**Figure 5.30**).

The markup tools available in Acrobat are illustrated in **Figure 5.31**. They are as follows, from top to bottom in the illustration:

◆ **Highlight Selected Text** adds a colored backdrop to the selected text to draw attention to it.

◆ **Insert Text at Cursor** indicates that text should be inserted into the existing words. A little caret appears at the place you click in the text. The pop-up window associated with the annotation contains the new text.

◆ **Crossout Text for Deletion** lines out the selected text, indicating that it should be removed.

◆ **Replace Selected Text** lines out the selected text, indicating that it should be removed, and places an insert-text caret at the end, indicating that new text should be inserted. The pop-up window associated with the annotation contains the new text.

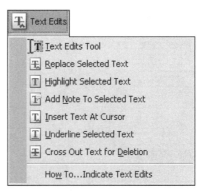

Figure 5.30 The text markup tools reside in the Text Edits menu in the Comment & Markup toolbar.

Figure 5.31 Acrobat provides all the tools you need to do full text markup on an Acrobat file.

Figure 5.32 Acrobat provides shortcut tools for highlighting, underlining, and crossing out text. Unfortunately, only highlighting exists in the Comment & Markup toolbar by default.

◆ **Add Note to Selected Text** highlights the text. The pop-up window associated with the annotation contains a comment about the text. This seems to be in every way identical to the Highlight Text tool, except that Acrobat automatically opens the pop-up window so you can type your comment.

◆ **Underline Selected Text** underlines the text for emphasis.

To add a text markup to a page:

1. Click the Text Edit tool (not its drop-down menu) in the Comment & Markup toolbar.

The mouse pointer turns into an I-beam.

2. If you're indicating an insertion point, click a location in the text on the page.

A blinking cursor appears at that point on the page.

3. For all other types of edits, select the text that you want to mark up.

Acrobat highlights the text. You may use the Shift key to extend the selection, as is usual in word processors.

4. In the menu attached to the Text Edits tool (Figure 5.30), select the markup you want.

Acrobat immediately applies the markup. If your markup requires insertion or notation text, a pop-up window opens so you can type your text.

✔ Tip

■ The Comment & Markup toolbar can contain tools that allow you to quickly highlight, underline, and cross out text (**Figure 5.32**). Unfortunately, only the Highlight Text tool is in the toolbar by default; see Chapter 1 for directions on adding the other two.

TEXT EDITS

Applying a Stamp to the Page

One of the most popular annotation types (well, *I* like it) is the Stamp tool. This comment type is modeled on the traditional rubber stamp once popular with banks and still popular with 4-year-old children.

The Stamps are available from the Stamp drop-down menu in the Comment & Markup toolbar (**Figure 5.33**).

The Stamps are organized into categories: Dynamic, Sign Here, and business are provided by default. You can also compile your own Favorites menu, containing Stamps you particularly like.

Furthermore, Acrobat thinks of the most recently used Stamp as the current Stamp and places it at the top of the Stamp menu (**Figure 5.34**) for convenient access.

Note that some of the Stamps are dynamic, incorporating the identity data you supplied when you first started using the comment tools (**Figure 5.35**).

You can create your own Stamps and your own categories. The Acrobat version of a Stamp allows you to use any PDF graphic—any combination of text, line art, and images—as your rubber stamp. You'll see how to do this in the next section.

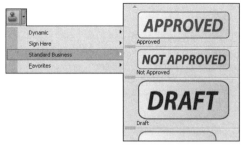

Figure 5.33 The Stamp tool lets you place predefined graphics on the page as the equivalent of a rubber stamp.

Figure 5.34 The Stamp you most recently used resides at the top of the Stamp menu as the current stamp.

Figure 5.35 Dynamic Stamps incorporate information from your system and personal identity data.

Figure 5.36 Having selected a Stamp in the Stamp menu, you move a ghostly version of it to the correct location on the page.

Figure 5.37 Clicking a Stamp yields handles you can use to resize it.

To apply a Stamp to the page:

1. In the Stamp tool menu (Figure 5.33), choose the category and Stamp you want.

   The mouse pointer turns into a ghostly version of the stamp you choose, like the Draft Stamp in **Figure 5.36**.

2. Click at the place on the page where you want your Stamp to go.

   Acrobat places the Stamp on the page in its default size.

3. Click the Stamp image on the page to select it.

   Handles appear at the corners of the Stamp (**Figure 5.37**).

4. Click and drag the handles to make the Stamp the size you want.

   Once you've used a Stamp, it becomes your current Stamp and is convenient to use again. Just click the Stamp tool button (not the drop-down menu) and place the Stamp on the page as described.

Creating Your Own Stamp

It is remarkably easy to create your own Stamp for use with the Stamp tool. You can take graphics, text, or images from any PDF file and turn them into a Stamp.

You can even create new categories for your Stamps.

To create a stamp:

1. In the Stamp tool's menu, select Create Custom Stamp (**Figure 5.38**).

   Acrobat will present you with the Select Image for Custom Stamp dialog box (**Figure 5.39**).

2. Click the Browse button.

   The standard Open dialog box opens.

3. Choose the file that contains the artwork you want to use for a Stamp.

   This can be a PDF file or any type of file that Acrobat can convert to PDF. Acrobat displays the first page of the document in the dialog box.

4. Using the scroll bar, select the page in the document that you want to use as your Stamp.

5. Click OK.

   The Create Custom Stamp dialog box opens (**Figure 5.40**).

6. Choose a category to which to add your Stamp, or type in the name of a new category.

Figure 5.38 To create your own Stamp, select Create Custom Stamp from the Stamp menu.

Figure 5.39 Select a file as the source for your Stamp's graphic.

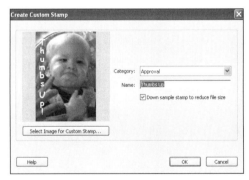

Figure 5.40 Give your new Stamp a name and assign it to a category. You may type in a new category name, if you wish.

Figure 5.41 Your new category and Stamp appear in the Stamp menu.

Figure 5.42 The Manage Custom Stamps dialog box lets you delete and edit existing custom Stamps and create new ones.

7. Type a name for your new Stamp.

8. Click OK.

Your new Stamp appears among the other Stamps in the Stamp tool menu (**Figure 5.41**).

✔ Tip

- If you don't expect to ever use your Stamp at a large size on the page, you can save some space on your disk by checking the "Down sample" check box in the Custom Stamp dialog box (Figure 5.40). This option can reduce your Stamp's size considerably, but it can also make your Stamp look chunky if you use the Stamp's handles to make it large.

Having created a custom stamp, you can remove it again using the Manage Custom Stamps dialog box (**Figure 5.42**).

To delete a custom Stamp:

1. In the Stamp tool's menu, select Manage Stamps.

Acrobat will display the Manage Custom Stamps dialog box.

2. In the list of Stamps, select the Stamp you want to delete.

Acrobat shows the Stamp's graphic in the dialog box.

3. Click Delete.

Acrobat deletes the custom Stamp.

4. Click OK.

✔ Tip

- Note from Figure 5.42 that you can also edit the selected Stamp (rename it and change its category) and create new Stamps.

Checking Spelling in Comments

Acrobat has a built-in spell-check feature that looks for spelling errors in a document's comments and form fields. The only difficulty in using this feature is finding it; it's located in a submenu that's otherwise unrelated to forms or commenting.

To check spelling in your comments:

1. Select Tools > Editing > Spell Check.

   The Check Spelling dialog box opens (**Figure 5.43**).

2. Click Start.

   Acrobat examines all the comments and form text fields in your document, looking for spelling errors. When it finds a misspelling, Acrobat presents the error in context and shows you a list of replacements (**Figure 5.44**).

3. For each misspelled word, do one of the following:

   ▲ Click Ignore to ignore that instance of the misspelled word.

   ▲ Click Ignore All to ignore all instances of that word.

   ▲ Choose a replacement in the list, and click either Change or Change All.

   ▲ Click Add to add the word to Acrobat's dictionary of known words.

   After you change, ignore, or add the misspelled word, Acrobat goes on to the next.

4. When there are no more misspellings, click Done.

Figure 5.43 Use the Check Spelling dialog box to check the spelling in your document's comments and form fields.

Figure 5.44 When Acrobat finds a misspelled word, it presents you with a list of alternatives.

Figure 5.45 Exporting comments results in an FDF file that contains only the document's comment data.

Exporting and Importing Comments

The data associated with a document's comments is much smaller than the document itself. A 10 MB PDF file may have less than 1 KB of comment data.

If someone sends you that 10 MB file for comment and you want to return the annotated file, it's more efficient to send just the comment data than it is to send the entire PDF file.

You do this by exporting the comments to a Form Data Format (FDF) file (**Figure 5.45**). This file contains only the text, images, position, and other data associated with your comments. You can email this relatively tiny file to another person; they can then import the FDF data into their copy of the same PDF file.

When Acrobat imports an FDF file, it places the comments into the new document in their original locations. This is a much more efficient way of sending comments from one location to another.

✔ Tip

- If you import an FDF file into a document that is *not* the same as the one you originally annotated, the imported comments won't correspond to the any particular text or graphic in the new document.

To export your comments to an FDF file:

1. Do one of the following, depending on your computer platform:
   - ▲ On the Macintosh, choose Comments > Export Comments (**Figure 5.46**).
   - ▲ In Windows, select Comments > Export Comments to Data File (**Figure 5.47**).

   Acrobat will present you with a standard Save-a-File dialog box.

2. Specify a name and location for your FDF file.

3. Click OK.

   Acrobat creates the FDF file.

✔ Tip

- ■ If you examine Figure 5.47, you'll see that you can also export PDF comments to a Microsoft Word or AutoCAD document. In this case, the PDF file you've annotated must have been originally created in Word or AutoCAD. The resulting file contains comments that may be imported into the original Word or AutoCAD document.

To import comments from an FDF file:

1. With the PDF file open, elect Comments > Import Comments.

   An Open dialog box opens.

2. Choose the FDF file that contains the comments.

   Acrobat reads the file and places the comments it contains into the current document.

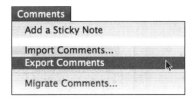

Figure 5.46 On the Macintosh, you select Comments > Export Comments.

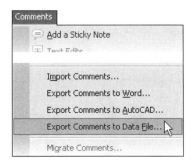

Figure 5.47 In Windows, you select Comments > Export Comments to Data File. Note that you can also export to Microsoft Word and AutoCAD.

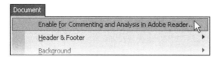

Figure 5.48 You must explicitly enable the use of Adobe Reader to comment on a document.

Figure 5.49 Acrobat warns you that once a document is enabled for commenting in Adobe Reader, it's no longer editable even in Acrobat Pro.

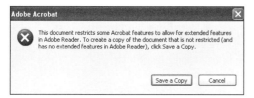

Figure 5.50 If you try to edit a Reader-enabled document in Acrobat Pro, you're prompted to save an editable copy of that document.

Enabling Commenting in Reader

Acrobat Pro Only: By default, PDF documents cannot be modified in any way with the free Adobe Reader. Unfortunately, this ban includes attaching comments to a file. If you want people to be able to review your document in Adobe Reader, you must explicitly turn on that ability for the document.

Once your PDF document has been enabled for commenting in Reader, you're restricted in what you can do to that document. Even in Acrobat Standard or Pro, you can no longer shuffle pages, edit page contents, add form fields or links, or otherwise modify the document. This will be true until you disable the ability to annotate the document in Reader.

To enable a document for commenting in Adobe Reader:

1. Select Document > Enable for Commenting and Analysis in Adobe Reader (**Figure 5.48**).

   Acrobat will present you with a dialog box warning you that file editing will be restricted (**Figure 5.49**). Then a Save dialog box opens, because Acrobat insists that you re-save the Reader-enabled file.

2. Save the Reader-enabled file with a new name and new location on your disk.

   If you later attempt to edit the PDF file in Acrobat Pro or Standard, an alert opens, giving you an opportunity to save a copy of the document without Adobe Reader commenting permission (**Figure 5.50**); the newly saved file is once again editable in Acrobat Pro.

READING COMMENTED DOCUMENTS

The previous chapter described how to annotate a PDF file with circles, arrows, and paragraphs of explanatory text. We covered how to mark up the text in your PDF files to indicate insertions, deletions, and replacements.

In this chapter, we discuss what to do when you receive such a marked-up document. Of course, you can always just double-click an annotation and read the text in the resulting pop-up window. However, Acrobat gives you several more-efficient ways of examining a document's annotations.

Let's see what they are.

Examining the Comments List

The Comments List is a navigation pane you can view by clicking the appropriate icon to the left of your document page (**Figure 6.1**). Unlike the other navigation panes, the Comments List displays across the bottom of the document window.

The Comments List itemizes all the comments in your document. It also has a toolbar across the top that provides easy access to a variety of tasks common to working with comments. This pane is invaluable when you're working with a document that has more than one or two comments.

Like all navigation panes, the Comments List pane can be dragged off the left edge of the document window to become a stand-alone palette (**Figure 6.2**).

Figure 6.1 The Comments List itemizes all the comments in your document.

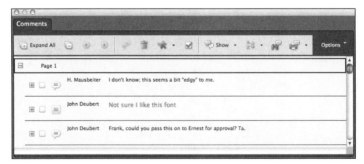

Figure 6.2 When you drag the Comments List away from the document window, it becomes a stand-alone floating palette.

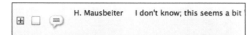

Figure 6.3 When collapsed, an entry in the Comments List shows a comment's author and text.

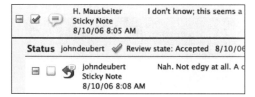

Figure 6.4 An expanded entry displays all the information for a comment, including any replies.

Figure 6.5 The Expand All and Collapse All buttons do just what their names imply.

Each entry in the Comments List has two states. Initially, the entry is collapsed, showing only the comment's author, date, and text (**Figure 6.3**).

The collapsed item has a Expand button, the boxed plus sign visible in Figure 6.3. When you click it, you see additional information associated with the comment. This can include the comment's status and any replies that have been made to that comment (**Figure 6.4**). Note in Figure 6.4 that the Expand button becomes a Collapse button—a minus sign in a box.

✔ Tip

■ I find it useful to use the Comments List as a palette. When it's docked to the bottom of the window, the list obscures too much of the document's page for my liking.

To expand and collapse entries in the Comments List:

1. Select the comment in which you're interested.

2. Click the Expand button to display that comment's additional information.

3. Click the Collapse button to hide the additional information.

The Comments List toolbar also has a pair of buttons (**Figure 6.5**) that will expand and collapse all of the entries in the list.

To expand and collapse all entries in the Comments List:

1. Click the Expand All button to expand all the comments in the list.

2. Click the Collapse All button to collapse all the comments in the list.

EXAMINING THE COMMENTS LIST

Replying to a Comment

Having read a comment, you may want to reply to it—answer a question posed in the comment, deny any wrongdoing implied by the comment, and so on.

Figure 6.6 Click the Reply to Comment icon to reply to a comment.

To reply to a comment in the Comments List:

1. Select the comment to which you want to reply.

2. Click the Reply to Comment icon in the toolbar (**Figure 6.6**).

   Acrobat expands the comment entry and adds a new line with a text box for your reply (**Figure 6.7**).

3. Type the text of your reply.

✔ Tip

■ You can also reply to a comment by right-clicking the comment's icon and selecting Reply in the contextual menu.

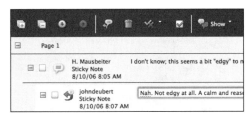

Figure 6.7 When you click the Reply to Comment button, Acrobat expands the comment entry and gives you space to type your reply.

Figure 6.8 The Review submenu of the Set Status tool lets you assign a status state to a comment.

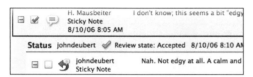

Figure 6.9 A comment's status state is among the information displayed when you expand a comment's entry.

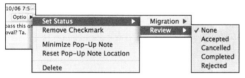

Figure 6.10 You can also set a comment's status state from its pop-up window.

Figure 6.11 Each comment entry has a check box whose significance is up to you.

✔ **Tip**

■ You can also check-mark a comment by right-clicking the comment's icon and selecting Mark with Checkmark in the contextual menu. This menu item becomes Remove Checkmark if the comment is already checked.

Marking Comments

The Comments List toolbar lets you indicate that you have reviewed a comment. Setting a comment's review status indicates that you have come to some decision regarding that comment, such as accepting it as true or rejecting it as an outright lie.

To set the review status of a comment:

1. Select the comment in the Comments List.

2. In the Comments List toolbar, select the Set Status tool (**Figure 6.8**).

   A menu drops down from the tool.

3. In the Review submenu, select the status you want for this comment.

   The comment's new status appears in the Comments List (**Figure 6.9**).

✔ Tips

■ You can also set the review status of a comment from the Option menu in the comment's pop-up window, as in **Figure 6.10**.

■ Acrobat provides five review status values: None, Accepted, Cancelled, Completed, and Rejected. The precise meaning of these status values is up to the reviewer. Acrobat doesn't define the difference between, for example, Cancelled and Rejected.

Each comment in the Comments List has a check box whose significance is up to the reviewer (**Figure 6.11**). If you were keeping track of which comments mention bunnies, you could set each comment's checkmark as you encounter a "bunny" reference.

To set or clear a comment's checkmark

◆ Click the comment's check box.

   This action toggles the checked state; it turns on if it was off and vice versa.

Managing the Comments List

The Comments List toolbar gives you considerable control over which comments it displays and how it displays them. In this section you'll see how to modify the visibility of items in the Comments List.

The Show tool (**Figure 6.12**) lets you choose which comments you want to appear on the PDF page and in the Comments List. The menu attached to this tool consists of a series of submenus allowing you to choose visible comments by type, reviewer, status, and whether the comment is checked.

Each submenu allows you to choose among the available comment types, reviewers, and so on. Note in Figure 6.12 that you can have multiple selections scattered among the submenus. You can choose to see all the Notes and Text Editing Markups from reviewer Quentin P. Fonebotham, for example.

To choose which comments should be visible:

1. In the Comments List toolbar, click the Show tool (Figure 6.12).

2. Choose the type, review, status, or checked state you want to make visible in the Comments list.

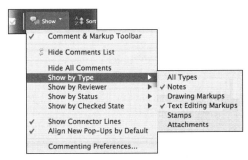

Figure 6.12 You may select among a variety of criteria to determine which comments are displayed on the page and in the Comments List.

Figure 6.13 You can sort the Comments List several ways.

If you want to make all the comments visible again, there is a bit of a trick to it. The "Show All Comments" item in the Show tool's menu is not available unless all the document's comments are hidden.

To make all comments visible:

1. In the Show menu, select Hide All Comments.

   All comments in the document disappear, and the Show All Comments item appears in the Show tool menu.

2. In the Show tool menu, select Show All Comments.

   All of the document's comments become visible.

The Comments List toolbar allows you to sort the comments in the list by a variety of criteria, including type, page number, and author.

To sort the items in the Comments List:

1. In the Comments List toolbar, click the Sort By tool (**Figure 6.13**).

   A menu drops down from the tool button.

2. Select the criterion by which you want to sort the comments.

   The list will immediately redraw itself in the new order.

MANAGING THE COMMENTS LIST

Searching for Text in Comments

The Comments List allows you to search for words or phrases in the document's comments. The process is much like searching for text in the PDF file as a whole.

Figure 6.14 The Search tool allows you to search for a word or phrase in a document's comments.

To search for a word among a document's comments:

1. In the Comments List toolbar, click the Search tool (**Figure 6.14**).

   Acrobat resizes your document window and opens the Search window next to it (**Figure 6.15**). The two windows together take up the entire screen. (This can be disconcerting the first time you see it.)

2. Type the word or phrase for which you want to search into the Search window.

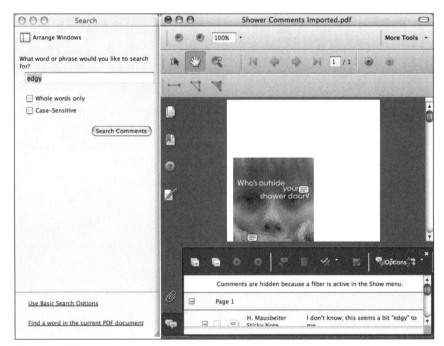

Figure 6.15 When you click the Search tool, Acrobat resizes your document window and displays the Search window.

Figure 6.16 The Search window displays all the comments in your document that contain the target phrase.

3. Click the Search Comments button.

Acrobat searches through your comments and returns a list of hits in the Search window (**Figure 6.16**).

4. To view one of the found comments, click its entry in the hit list.

Acrobat highlights that comment in the document window, changing pages as needed.

5. To do another search, click the New Search button in the Search dialog box and then repeat steps 2–4.

6. To finish searching, click the Search window's standard Close control (the red button on the Mac or the X button in Windows).

Acrobat closes the Search window and returns the document window to its original size and position on the screen.

Printing Comments

You can print the comments in a document two ways:

◆ Print the PDF file as usual, with the comments in place on the printed pages.

◆ Print a summary of the comments, printing the comment text and, optionally, a reduced image of each document page showing where the comment occurs in the document.

To print a PDF file with comments in place:

1. Select File > Print.

Acrobat will present you with the Print dialog box (**Figure 6.17**).

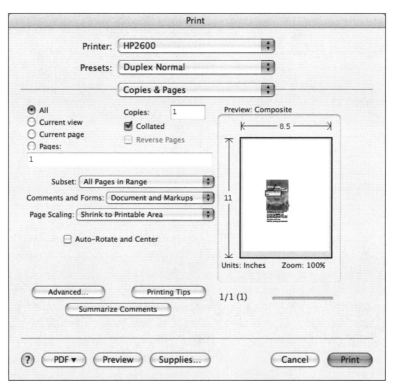

Figure 6.17 The Print dialog box lets you print your document together with its comments.

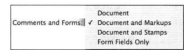

Figure 6.18 You can print the document and either its markups or its stamps.

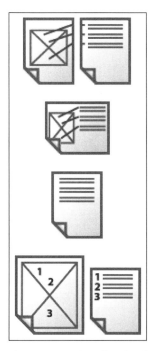

Figure 6.19 Acrobat offers four formats for printing a summary of a document's comments.

2. In the Comments and Forms pop-up menu (**Figure 6.18**), select one of the following:

   ▲ To print the document and annotations other than stamps, choose Document and Markups.

   ▲ To print the document and stamps, choose Document and Stamps.

   You can't print both markups and stamps; I don't know why.

3. Click Print.

   Acrobat prints the document and annotations.

Summarizing comments

Acrobat can also print a summary of all the comments in the document. It can print the summary in one of four formats (**Figure 6.19**):

◆ Each document page alternating with a page of comment text. Lines connect the comment text to the corresponding place on the document page when the pages are placed side by side (**Figure 6.20**).

◆ A thumbnail of each page printed side-by-side on a single page with the comment text for that page. Lines connect each comment with the corresponding position on the document page.

continues on next page

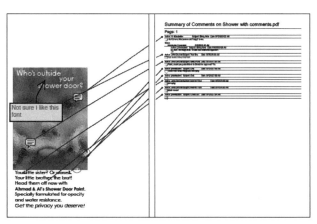

Figure 6.20 Most of the summary formats print each comment's text and indicate its position on the document page.

PRINTING COMMENTS

◆ A list of all the comment text, sorted by page number.

◆ Each document page alternating with a page of comment text. Each comment is numbered, and a corresponding number is placed at the comment's position on the document page.

To print a summary of a document's comments:

1. In the Comments List toolbar, click the Print Comments tool.

A menu drops down from the tool (**Figure 6.21**).

2. Select Print Comments Summary.

The Summarize Options dialog box opens (**Figure 6.22**).

3. Select the radio button corresponding to the type of summary you want.

4. Click Print Comment Summary.

Acrobat prints the comment summary.

✔ Tip

■ If you select Create PDF of Comments Summary in the Print Comments menu (Figure 6.21), Acrobat creates a PDF file of the summary in the format you've chosen, rather than printing the summary on the page.

Figure 6.21 You can print a comment summary on paper or save it as a PDF file.

Figure 6.22 The Summarize Options dialog box lets you select the format you want for the summary.

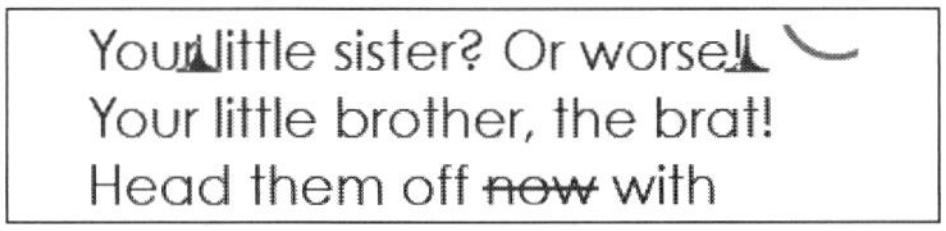

Youd little sister? Or worsed ⌐ ⌐
Your little brother, the brat!
Head them off ~~now~~ with

Figure 6.23 This text has a variety of markups added to it.

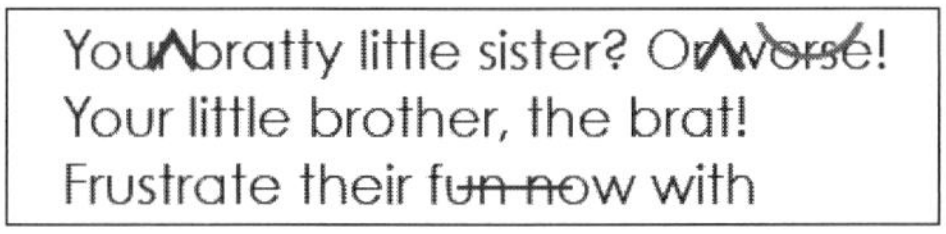

Youд bratty little sister? Or worse!
Your little brother, the brat!
Frustrate their ~~fun now~~ with

Figure 6.24 Importing the markups from Figure 6.23 into a revised version of the PDF file results in many of the markups no longer lining up with the original text.

Migrating Comments

In the previous chapter, we discussed importing comments from an FDF file into a PDF document. The imported comments are placed onto the document's pages in their original locations—the same x and y coordinates as in the reviewer's copy of the file.

Unfortunately, if the PDF file has been revised since the review so it's no longer identical to the reviewer's copy, the imported comments may no longer line up with the text or graphic elements to which they pertain (**Figures 6.23** and **6.24**).

Migrating comments into the revised document, instead of importing them, solves this problem. With migration, Acrobat attempts to place each comment in the same position relative to the page's contents. Even if text has been reflowed, illustrations have moved to different pages, and images have been repositioned, the comments pertaining to those items still find their proper targets.

Migrating comments has a requirement, however: Both the commented and the revised versions of the PDF file must be *tagged*. A tagged PDF file contains internal information identifying significant part of the document structure: paragraphs of text, graphics, chapter titles, and so on. Some applications, such as Adobe InDesign, place tags into the PDF files they create; most don't. Acrobat can add tags to PDF files that are missing them.

To tag a PDF file for comment migration:

◆ Select Advanced > Accessibility > Add Tags to Document.

To migrate comments into a modified PDF file:

1. Select Comments > Migrate Comments.

   The Migrate Comments dialog box opens (**Figure 6.25**).

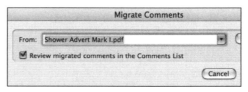

Figure 6.25 You migrate comments from the reviewer's copy of the PDF file.

2. Select the file to be tagged by doing one of the following:

   ▲ From the drop-down menu, choose a PDF file that's currently open.

   ▲ Click the Choose button, and select a PDF file on your disk.

3. Click OK.

   Acrobat analyzes the PDF file, placing tags into the file. Acrobat may also report any problems it had interpreting the document's structure.

   Acrobat reads the comments in the file you selected, placing them in the appropriate place on the current documents pages.

REVIEWING
PDF DOCUMENTS

Previous chapters have discussed Acrobat's tools for placing and reading comments on a PDF page. The techniques that those chapters covered are excellent for soliciting comments from two or three other people.

However, what if you're conducting a company-wide review of a document? You may be sending the PDF file to a dozen people to get comments and critiques. How do you keep track of the people to whom you have sent the document for review? And once you start receiving the annotated files back from the reviewers, how will you handle all the comments? Read them side by side? Import them into a single PDF file so you can look at them all at once?

Acrobat makes it relatively easy to conduct a broadly distributed review of a document. Acrobat will manage the process for you, sending copies of the document to reviewers and then collecting all their comments into a single copy of the file.

Acrobat can deliver copies to reviewers in two ways: emailing the document to all the reviewers (an *email-based review*) or arranging a server-based distribution across corporate network (a *shared review*).

You'll see how to do both of these.

Starting an Email-Based Review

In an email-based review, Acrobat emails copies of a document to several reviewers. When reviewers open the received document, they comment on the document using the standard Acrobat annotation tools and then return the document by email. When the author opens the returned, annotated copy, Acrobat merges the comments into the author's original PDF file. Eventually, the original file contains the comments returned by all the reviewers.

To start an email-based review:

1. In the Tasks toolbar, choose Send for Review > Send by Email for Review (**Figure 7.1**).

    Acrobat displays the first step in the Send by Email for Review Wizard (**Figure 7.2**), which gives an overview of the process.

2. Click the Choose button, and choose the PDF file to be reviewed.

    As a convenience, you may choose an open PDF document in the pop-up menu.

3. Click Next.

    Acrobat displays the second step in the Send by Email for Review Wizard, which allows you to invite reviewers (**Figure 7.3**).

4. Type the email addresses of the reviewers into the text box.

    You can separate reviewers' email addresses with spaces, semicolons, or new lines.

    You may instead click the Address Book button and select people in your system's address book.

Figure 7.1 You initiate a review by choosing Send by Email for Review on the Tasks toolbar.

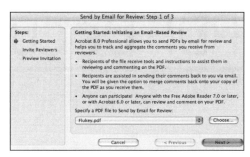

Figure 7.2 The first step in the Send by Email for Review Wizard specifies the file that is to be reviewed.

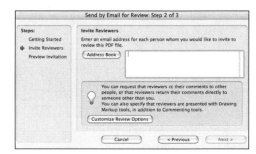

Figure 7.3 The second step in the Wizard is to supply the email addresses of all the reviewers.

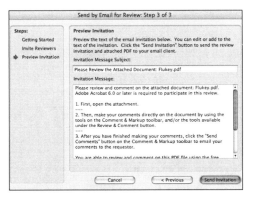

Figure 7.4 You finish by editing the subject and message text of the notification emails.

Figure 7.5 When you're invited to review a document, the PDF file is attached to the email.

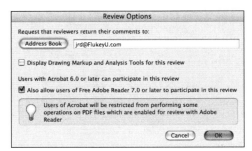

Figure 7.6 When setting up the email-based review, you can allow users to review the document using Adobe Reader.

5. Click Next.

Acrobat displays the final step in the Send by Email for Review Wizard (**Figure 7.4**), which lets you read and modify, if you wish, the email the reviewers will see.

6. Type the text that you want for your email's subject in the Invitation Message Subject field.

7. Modify or replace the email's message text as you wish.

In most cases, you should leave the message text as is, because it provides detailed directions to the reviewers on what to do.

8. Click the Send Invitation button.

Acrobat launches your email client and displays the outbound mail message with the PDF file attached (**Figure 7.5**).

9. Click your email client's Send button or otherwise send the email message on its way.

✔ Tips

■ Depending on your computer setup, you may not see your email client. In particular, the Windows version of Acrobat may send the email messages directly.

■ Acrobat Pro Only: If you want reviewers to be able to comment on your document using Adobe Reader, click Customize Review Options in the second step of the Send by Email wizard (Figure 7.3). The resulting Review Options dialog box (**Figure 7.6**) has a check box that enables Adobe Reader commentary.

■ The same Review Options dialog box also lets you supply an alternative return email address.

Reviewing a Document

When you receive a document for review, you get an email—in your usual email software—with the PDF file attached. When you open that PDF file, Acrobat recognizes that it's part of a review and automatically does three things that make it easy to review the document:

◆ Makes the Comment & Markup toolbar visible

◆ Adds a Send Comments button to the toolbar (**Figure 7.7**)

◆ Adds to the top of the document pane helpful instructions on how what to do with the document (**Figure 7.8**)

To review a PDF document:

1. Open the PDF file attached to the notification email.

   If this email was sent to you by another reviewer, the Merge Comments dialog box asks if you want to see the other person's comments (**Figure 7.9**).

2. If you are presented with the Merge Comments dialog box, click Yes or No, according to whether you want to see other people's comments.

   Acrobat displays the document in a window with the review instructions, as in Figure 7.8.

3. Make your comments on the document as described in Chapter 5.

4. When you're finished annotating the document, click the Send Comments button.

   The Send Comments dialog box opens (**Figure 7.10**).

5. Click the Send button.

   Acrobat launches your email client and displays the outbound mail message with the PDF file attached.

6. Click your email client's Send button or otherwise send the email message on its way.

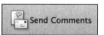

Figure 7.7 A reviewer can return the commented PDF file by clicking the Send Comments button in the Comment & Markup toolbar.

Figure 7.8 Acrobat presents the reviewer with instructions on how to review the emailed document.

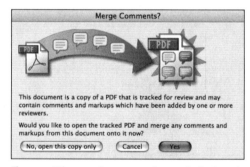

Figure 7.9 When a reviewer opens the email attachment, Acrobat offers to display any comments placed in the file by other reviewers.

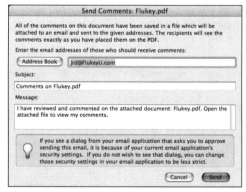

Figure 7.10 When the reviewer clicks Send Comments, Acrobat provides a chance to alter the return email's subject and message texts.

REVIEWING A DOCUMENT

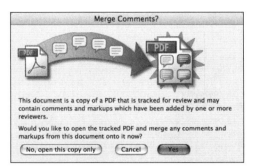

Figure 7.11 When the author opens a reviewed copy of the document, Acrobat offers to merge the comments into the original PDF file.

Figure 7.12 Acrobat merges the reviewer's comments into the original document file.

Receiving Email-Reviewed Documents

When you receive a reviewed copy of your document, the annotated version of the PDF file is attached to the notification email. Open this attached document, and Acrobat merges the comments it contains into your original copy.

To receive a reviewed document:

1. In your email software, open the attached PDF file.

    Acrobat will present you with the Merge Comments dialog box (**Figure 7.11**), which asks if you want to merge the comments into your copy of the document.

2. Click the Yes button.

    Acrobat opens the original PDF document and imports the comments from the attached PDF file into your original (**Figure 7.12**).

3. Read the comments as described in Chapter 6.

Starting a Shared Review

Shared reviews are technically more efficient than email-based reviews, because all the comments are stored in a single location rather than being shuttled around attached to different copies of the document. It may also be more appropriate if the file being reviewed is very large, because many email servers won't send or accept attachments that exceed some maximum size. (Five MB is a typical limit.)

The disadvantage of shared reviews is that all reviewers must have access to the same server, because that is where their comments will be stored. However, this is often the case in an office environment.

Before you can start a shared review, you must allocate a *comments repository*: a server location in which review comments are stored. This may be a folder on a server volume, a WebDAV folder, or a SharePoint workspace; the last two must be set up by your organization's system support staff.

For now, we'll set up a folder on a server volume as the repository for review documents, because you can do so without IT support.

To set up a comments repository:

1. Open Acrobat's Preferences by choosing (on the Macintosh) Acrobat > Preferences or (in Windows) Edit > Preferences.

   The Preferences dialog box opens.

2. Click the Reviewing category.

   Acrobat displays the controls for the Reviewing options (**Figure 7.13**).

3. In the Server Type pop-up menu, choose Network Folder.

4. Click the Choose button to choose a repository folder.

   The standard Open dialog box opens.

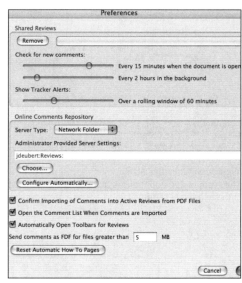

Figure 7.13 The Preferences dialog box allows you to establish a location for the comments repository.

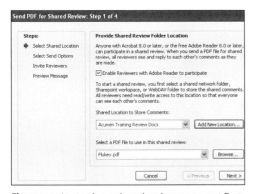

Figure 7.14 In starting a shared review, you must first specify the repository for the comments and the PDF file to be reviewed.

5. Choose a folder on your server volume; this will become your repository folder.

6. Click OK to close the Preferences dialog box.

✔ Tips

■ The other Reviewing preferences can be safely left alone. The only controls you may want to adjust are the sliders in the top half of the dialog box that specify how often Acrobat checks the server for the presence of new comments. I think the default values are reasonable, but if you're anxious, you may want Acrobat to check the server more often.

■ A single comments repository can be used for many reviews. Acrobat keeps track of which comments correspond to which reviews.

To start a shared review:

1. In the Comment & Markup toolbar, choose Send for Review > Send for Shared Review. Acrobat displays the first pane of the Send PDF for Shared Review Wizard, which records server information (**Figure 7.14**).

2. From the Shared Location to Store Comments pop-up menu, choose the comments repository you set up earlier in the Preferences.

3. Select a PDF file to be reviewed. You may choose among open PDF files in the pop-up menu or click the Browse button to select a file on your disk.

4. Acrobat Pro Only: If you want to allow reviewers to use Adobe Reader to comment on the document, click the Enable Reviewers with Adobe Reader check box.

   Note that you're restricted in your ability to edit the PDF file as long as Adobe Reader commenting is enabled.

continues on next page

SHARING A SHARED REVIEW

5. Click the Next button.

Acrobat displays the second pane of the Send for Shared Review Wizard, which determines how to send the document (**Figure 7.15**). The default values in this pane may be accepted as reasonable values.

6. Click Next.

Acrobat displays the third pane of the Send for Shared Review Wizard, which lets you invite reviewers (**Figure 7.16**).

7. Type the email addresses of the reviewers into the text box.

You can separate reviewers' email addresses with spaces, semicolons, or new lines.

Note that you can distinguish between reviewers who *must* review the document and those who are optional.

As a convenience, you may instead click the Address Book button and select people in your system's address book.

8. If you wish to set a deadline for the review, click the Set Deadline check box and enter a date into the month, day, and year fields.

9. Click Next.

Acrobat displays the final pane of the Send for Shared Review Wizard, where you can check out the invitation (**Figure 7.17**).

10. Edit the email subject and message content as you wish.

Note that in most cases, the default message text is most useful, because it gives instructions for how to review the document.

11. Click Finish.

Acrobat posts the PDF file to the server folder and notifies the reviewers by email.

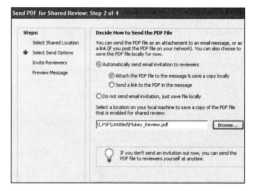

Figure 7.15 You must decide how the reviewed document will be sent to the reviewers. The defaults for these controls can be accepted.

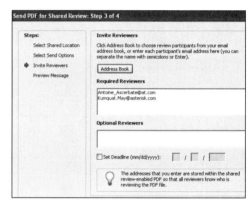

Figure 7.16 You must provide the email addresses of the reviewers.

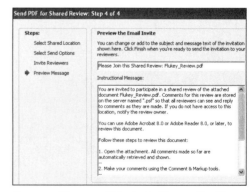

Figure 7.17 You can edit the text of the email subject and message.

SHARING A SHARED REVIEW

Reviewing a Shared Document

When you receive an emailed request for a shared review, the PDF document is attached to the email message. When you open this attachment, Acrobat will display the document together with all the currently existing comments downloaded from the comments repository. There is also a set of instructions at the top of the document pane (**Figure 7.18**) telling you how to proceed with the review.

Note that you must be connected to the server that holds the comments repository to review the document.

To review a server-based document:

1. In your email software, open the attached PDF file.

   Acrobat opens the document, together with any existing comments.

2. Add your comments to the document, using the comment tools as usual.

3. Click the Publish Comments link at the top of the document window (Figure 7.18).

   Acrobat stores your comments on the server.

✔ Tip

■ The comments you see on the document page were retrieved from the server when you opened the document. You can see comments that have been newly added by other reviewers by clicking the Check for New Comments link at the top of the document page (Figure 7.18).

Figure 7.18 When a reviewer opens a document for review, Acrobat adds several controls to the standard document window: Instructions on how to review the document, Check for New Comments link, Publish Comments link, Review & Comment toolbar menu.

REVIEWING A SHARED DOCUMENT

Receiving Server-Based Reviews

The best way to collect comments from a shared review is to use the Review Tracker (**Figure 7.19**). This tool lists all the reviews that you've initiated and lets you conveniently see the current state of all their comments.

Figure 7.19 Clicking a review server in the Review Tracker lists all the outstanding reviews on that server.

To read comments from a server-based review:

1. In the Comment & Markup toolbar, choose Send for Review > Tracker.

   Acrobat will present you with the Review Tracker dialog box (Figure 7.19).

2. Click the review server that contains the review you want to examine.

   The right side of the dialog box lists all the reviews on that server, as in Figure 7.19. (The figure shows only one entry: Flukey_Review.pdf.)

3. Click the review you want to examine.

   The "Welcome back to Shared Review" dialog box opens (**Figure 7.20**), which summarizes activity since the last time you looked at that review.

4. Click OK.

   Acrobat opens the PDF file and loads the reviewers' comments from the server (**Figure 7.21**).

5. View the comments in the document as discussed in Chapter 6.

✔ Tip

- Notice the Publish Comments link in Figure 7.21. It gives the review initiator the ability to publish new comments back to the server. This way, you can respond to comments and push the responses up to the server for others to see.

Figure 7.20 When the author checks on a shared review, Acrobat displays recent activity for that review.

Figure 7.21 When the author opens a reviewed document, Acrobat displays all the comments in the comments repository.

MANIPULATING PAGES

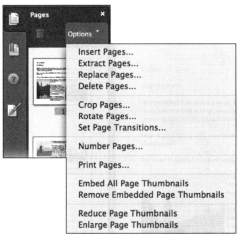

Figure 8.1 The page-manipulation commands are available in the Pages pane's Options menu.

Document	
Header & Footer	▶
Background	▶
Watermark	▶
Insert Pages...	⇧⌘I
Extract Pages...	
Replace Pages...	
Delete Pages...	⇧⌘D
Crop Pages...	⇧⌘T
Rotate Pages...	⇧⌘R

Figure 8.2 The commands are also available in the Acrobat Document menu.

Acrobat makes it easy to insert, delete, rearrange, and otherwise change the order of pages within a document.

You can get to these features in three ways:

◆ Click the Options button at the top of the Pages navigation pane (**Figure 8.1**). Acrobat displays a menu that contains all the page-manipulation commands.

◆ Right-click a thumbnail in the Pages navigation pane. The resulting contextual menu is identical to the Options menu.

◆ Go to Acrobat's Document menu (**Figure 8.2**), which has entries for the same commands.

I tend to find it most convenient to use Options button in the Pages navigation pane. You may prefer the other methods, and you have my permission to use them.

Rearranging Pages

You can move pages around in a PDF file using the Pages navigation pane; simply drag pages from their original locations to the places you want them.

To move a page from one location to another:

1. Click the Pages tab to open the Pages navigation pane.

2. Click the thumbnail of the page you want to move.

   Acrobat draws an outline around the thumbnail, indicating that the page is selected (**Figure 8.3**).

3. Drag the selected thumbnail to its new position in the document.

   As you drag the page, Acrobat places a short, light-colored line between existing thumbnails, indicating where the page will be placed; this is visible at the mouse pointer in **Figure 8.4**.

4. Release the mouse button.

   Acrobat moves the selected page to its new location (**Figure 8.5**).

✔ Tip

■ You can select more than one thumbnail in the Pages pane. Acrobat follows the conventional mouse-click rules in this pane: Shift-click selects a contiguous range of thumbnails; Command-click/Ctrl-click selects a noncontiguous set of pages.

Figure 8.3 When you select a thumbnail in the Pages pane, Acrobat highlights the thumbnail with a light blue outline.

Figure 8.4 As you drag a page in the Pages pane, a line indicates the page's new location.

Figure 8.5 Releasing the mouse button moves the page to its new location.

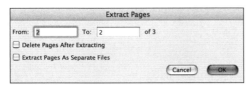

Figure 8.6 In the Extract Pages dialog box, you specify the range of pages you want to extract.

Extracting Pages

You can extract a range of pages from a PDF file and create a new PDF document from those pages. You can place all the extracted pages into a single PDF file or have Acrobat create a separate PDF file for each page.

To extract a range of pages from a document:

1. With the document open, click the Pages tab to open the Pages navigation pane.

2. In the Pages pane's Options menu, choose Extract Pages.

    Acrobat presents you with the Extract Pages dialog box (**Figure 8.6**).

3. In the From and To fields, indicate the beginning and ending page numbers of the pages you want to extract.

4. If you want to remove those pages from the original document, check Delete Pages After Extracting.

5. If you want each extracted page to become a separate, one-page PDF document, check Extract Pages As Separate Files.

6. Click OK.

    Acrobat extracts the pages as you've specified. The extracted pages appear in a new window named "Pages from [original document].pdf."

✔ Tip

■ As an alternative, you can select a set of thumbnails in the Pages navigation pane, right-click one of the selected thumbnails, and select Extract Pages from the contextual menu. The Extract Pages dialog box opens with the page range already set to the pages you selected.

EXTRACTING PAGES

Inserting One File into Another

Acrobat makes it easy to insert the contents of another PDF file into your current document.

To insert pages from another file into a document:

1. With the document open, click the Pages tab to open the Pages navigation pane.

2. In the Pages pane's Options menu, select Insert Pages.

   The standard Open dialog box opens.

3. Select the file that contains the pages you want to insert, and click OK.

   Acrobat presents you with the Insert Pages dialog box (**Figure 8.7**).

4. Specify where in your document the new pages should be inserted.

   Using a combination of the Location pop-up menu and the radio buttons, you may select before or after the first page or last page, or a specific page number.

5. Click OK.

   Acrobat inserts the contents of the other file into your current document.

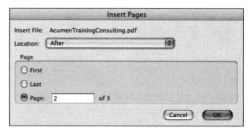

Figure 8.7 The Insert Pages dialog box specifies where the inserted pages should be placed.

Figure 8.8 The Replace Pages dialog box indicates which pages should be replaced and which page in the other document should replace them.

Replacing Pages

Acrobat allows you to replace a range of pages in the current document with pages taken from another PDF file.

To replace pages in your document:

1. With the document open, click the Pages tab to open the Pages navigation pane.

2. In the Pages pane's Options menu, select Replace Pages.

   The standard Open dialog box opens.

3. Select the file that contains the replacement pages, and click OK.

   The Replace Pages dialog box opens (**Figure 8.8**).

4. In the Original section, specify the range of pages that should be replaced.

5. In the Replacement section, specify the starting page number of the replacement pages in the other PDF file.

   Note that you don't need to specify an ending page number; the length of the replacement page range matches the number of pages you're replacing.

6. Click OK.

   Acrobat replaces the specified pages with pages taken from the other document.

Rotating Pages

When you export a landscape-oriented document from page-layout software or a word processor, Acrobat often displays the resulting pages sideways (**Figure 8.9**). The page is formatted landscape, but Acrobat displays it in portrait orientation.

This is easily fixed by having Acrobat rotate the pages in your document. Acrobat can rotate all the pages or a specified range of pages.

The pages will retain their new orientation in future viewings.

To rotate pages in the current document:

1. With the document open, click the Pages tab to open the Pages navigation pane.

2. In the Pages pane's Options menu, select Rotate Pages.

   The Rotate Pages dialog box opens (**Figure 8.10**).

   In the Direction pop-up menu (**Figure 8.11**), choose whether the pages should be rotated 90 degrees clockwise or counterclockwise, or a full 180 degrees.

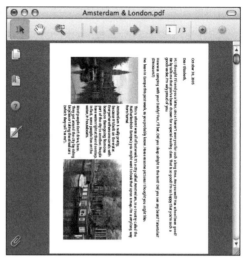

Figure 8.9 Many applications produce landscape pages that Acrobat displays in portrait orientation.

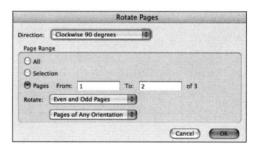

Figure 8.10 The Rotate Pages dialog box lets you specify which pages should be rotated and in what direction they should rotate.

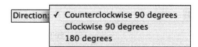

Figure 8.11 You may rotate pages 90 degrees clockwise or counterclockwise or a full 180 degrees.

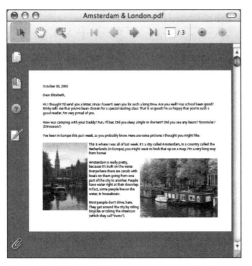

Figure 8.12 After rotation, your pages are oriented the way you want.

3. Using the radio buttons, select the range of pages you want to rotate:

▲ To rotate the entire document, choose All.

▲ To rotate pages you've selected in the Pages pane, choose Selection.

▲ To rotate a specific range of page numbers, choose Pages, and specify the beginning and ending page numbers.

4. In the Rotate pop-up menu, choose whether you want to rotate even pages, odd pages, or both.

5. In the unnamed pop-up menu below the Rotate pop-up menu, choose whether to rotate landscape pages, portrait pages, or both.

6. Click OK.

Acrobat rotates the pages you specified (**Figure 8.12**).

✔ Tip

■ Acrobat often uses the orientation of text on a page to determine whether that page is landscape or portrait. If you select a specific orientation in step 5, pages with no text on them may not be rotated, regardless of the actual orientation of the page.

ROTATING PAGES

Cropping Pages

Graphics applications often create PDF files whose pages have a lot of white space around the pages' contents (**Figure 8.13**). Acrobat lets you pare down the document page, cropping it so it contains only the content you want (**Figure 8.14**). You can also change the page dimensions to a standard size, such as Letter or A4.

Figure 8.13 Many graphics applications produce PDF pages with a lot of white space around the graphic.

To crop a page in a document:

1. With the document open to the page you want to crop, select Document > Crop Pages.

   Acrobat presents you with the Crop Pages dialog box (**Figure 8.15**).

Figure 8.14 You can crop pages so they contain only the part that is useful.

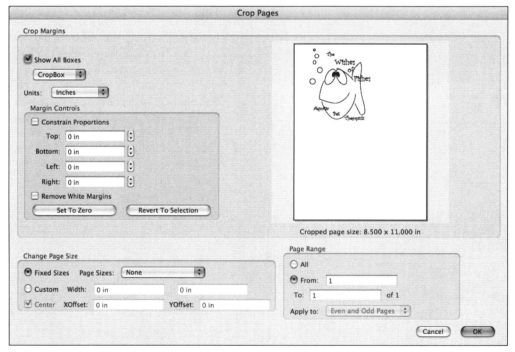

Figure 8.15 The Crop Pages dialog box lets you specify how much of the page should be trimmed from the left, right, top, and bottom of the page.

2. In the Margin Controls section, either enter values for the top, bottom, left, and right margins or click the arrows to increase or decrease the values of these margins (**Figure 8.16**).

   As you do so, Acrobat draws a rectangle showing you the present size of the page.

3. In the Page Range section, select the range of pages whose size you want to change.

   You can select a range of pages or choose All to crop all the pages. By default, the page range is set to include only the current page.

4. Click the OK button.

   Acrobat reduces the page size.

continues on next page

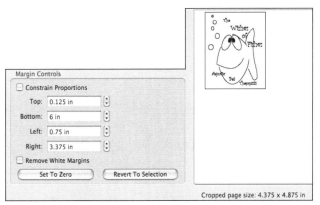

Figure 8.16 As you increase the margin sizes, Acrobat displays a rectangle in the preview picture, indicating the new page boundaries.

CROPPING PAGES

✔ Tips

■ Acrobat doesn't discard any content data when it crops a page. If you select the cropped page and return to the Crop Pages dialog box, you can click the Set To Zero button to recover the original page size.

■ You can select whatever unit of measure you wish from the Units pop-up menu. It offers points, picas, millimeters, centimeters, and inches. No furlongs, I'm afraid.

■ You can indicate units of measure for the margins by using abbreviations (pt, pc, mm, cm, in) in the margin size boxes, as in Figure 8.16.

■ The Crop Pages dialog box can be used to change the paper size of your document. Select the paper size (Letter, Legal, A4, and so on) from the Page Sizes menu. I often use this with scanned document pages, which never seem to come out exactly 8½ × 11 inches. I choose Letter for the page size and All for the page range, and all my image pages are resized.

■ The previous tip notwithstanding, don't be too extreme with the Change Page Size controls. Changing the page size can also change the proportion of your page contents (**Figure 8.17**).

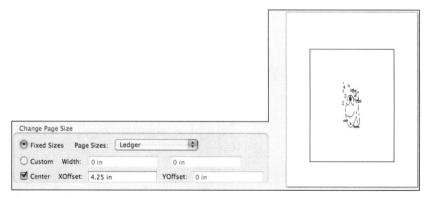

Figure 8.17 When you change paper size using Acrobat, you also change the proportions of the drawing.

CROPPING PAGES

ADDING AND CHANGING TEXT AND GRAPHICS

9

PDF isn't intended to be an editable document format. Adobe meant a PDF file to be a "snapshot" of a document as it was at a particular time.

Nonetheless, Acrobat breaks with that vision by providing extremely useful tools for *touching up* a document—making common changes that are convenient to some people and absolutely vital to others. This includes fixing typos, adding page numbers, and even modifying images using Adobe Photoshop or another editor of your choice.

In this chapter, we'll look at the most routinely useful tools for modifying a PDF document in Acrobat 8.

Touching Up Text

One of the first—and most requested—editing capabilities Adobe included in Acrobat was the ability to make minor changes to the text in a PDF file. This ability isn't intended for wholesale rewriting of text; rather, it lets you fix a wrong telephone number or add a missing comma. Before Adobe added this feature, even a minor typo would send you back to your original word-processor file, where you'd have to make the change and regenerate the PDF file.

When you select the TouchUp Text tool in the Advanced Editing toolbar (**Figure 9.1**), the mouse pointer becomes a text-editing I-beam whenever it roams over text (**Figure 9.2**). You edit text using the same techniques you use in a text editor: Click the text you want to change, and type your addition or replacement.

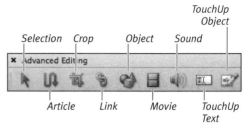

Figure 9.1 The Advanced Editing toolbar contains tools for manipulating and modifying documents.

Figure 9.2 With the TouchUp Text tool selected, you can select text on your PDF page.

To change text in a document:

1. Click the TouchUp Text tool in the Advanced Editing toolbar (Figure 9.1).

2. Either click the text to insert a change or select text that you want to delete or replace.

   Acrobat inserts a blinking cursor at the place you clicked or highlights the text you selected (Figure 9.2).

3. Type the text you want to insert into the PDF file.

✔ Tips

■ Acrobat implements all the standard key commands for moving the blinking cursor to the next word, the end of the line, and so on.

■ To replace or add text, that text's font must be installed in your computer system.

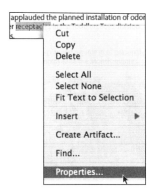

Figure 9.3 Right-clicking text with the TouchUp Text tool yields a contextual menu with access to text properties.

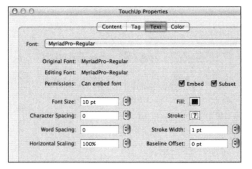

Figure 9.4 The TouchUp Properties dialog box lets you change the font, size, and other characteristics of the selected text.

In addition to inserting and deleting text, the TouchUp Text tool lets you change the font, size, alignment, and other properties of text in your PDF file.

To change text properties:

1. Click the TouchUp Text tool in the Advanced Editing toolbar.

2. Select the text whose properties you want to change.

   Right-click the text to display a contextual menu (**Figure 9.3**).

3. Choose Properties.

   Acrobat presents you with the TouchUp Properties dialog box (**Figure 9.4**).

4. Choose a font from the pop-up menu.

5. If you select a font, also choose the Embed and Subset check boxes.

   These options embed the font in the PDF file, ensuring that the text will look the same on other computers.

6. Type a font size into the Font Size field, or click the tiny up and down arrows to increase or decrease the font size.

7. Click Close.

✔ Tip

■ The TouchUp properties dialog box does let you change a number of other properties, including word spacing and horizontal offset. These can be occasionally useful for adjusting the appearance of your text.

Modifying Line Art

Acrobat Pro Only: There are two ways you can change lines, rectangles, and other line art on an Acrobat page. Acrobat provides a TouchUp Object tool that lets you change the position and orientation of graphic objects on the page. For extensive changes, Acrobat lets you edit page contents in Adobe Illustrator or another graphics editor; Illustrator is the default.

Keep in mind that we're talking about graphic objects that are part of the page content, not the lines, rectangles, and other graphics that can be associated with a comment.

Let's start by looking at the Acrobat tools.

Changing an object's position and size:

1. Click the TouchUp Object tool in the Advanced Editing toolbar.

2. Click a graphic object on the document page.

   Acrobat draws a rectangle around the object to indicate that it's selected (**Figure 9.5**).

3. To change the object's size, click and drag one of the handles at the square's corners.

4. To reposition the object, click and drag it to the desired position (**Figure 9.6**).

✔ Tips

■ Holding down the Shift key as you drag an object constrains your motion to angles of 90 degrees from the original position.

■ In contrast, when you resize an object, Acrobat normally preserves the object's original shape, scaling the object identically in the horizontal and vertical directions. To release this constraint, hold down the Shift key while you drag the object's handles; Acrobat lets you drag that handle anywhere you wish, scaling the horizontal and vertical dimensions separately.

Figure 9.5 A bounding rectangle signifies that you've selected an object with the TouchUp Object tool.

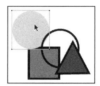

Figure 9.6 You can drag objects around the page with the TouchUp Objects tool. Note that the fill and border of an object are often separate.

Selecting Fill and Border

A graphic object may reside in a PDF file as two objects, one each for the fill and the border. In that case, the TouchUp Object tool may choose only one of the two objects.

If that is the case for the object you're editing, you need to either move the two objects separately or choose both at once by dragging out a marquee with the TouchUp Object tool (**Figure 9.7**). This marquee must touch the outline of the object to choose both the fill and border; it doesn't need to completely enclose the object. Then you can move or resize both the fill and the border of the object.

Figure 9.7 To choose both the fill and border of an object, drag a marquee with the TouchUp Object tool that intersects the object's border.

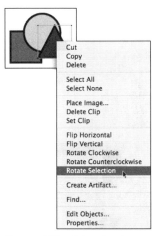

Figure 9.8 To rotate artwork on the PDF page, right-click an object and choose Rotate Selection.

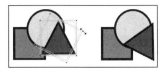

Figure 9.9 Having chosen Rotate Selection, you can drag one of the handles at the bounding box's corners to rotate the object.

Right-clicking a graphic object with the TouchUp Object tool yields a contextual menu (**Figure 9.8**) that lets you flip or rotate objects. Simply choose the appropriate command from the menu. The menu commands are generally straightforward; one item that may be tricky is rotating by an arbitrary amount.

To rotate an object by an arbitrary amount:

1. Click the TouchUp Object tool in the Advanced Editing toolbar.

2. Click a graphic object to select it.

Note that if the object consists of separate fill and border objects, you need to select both by dragging a marquee.

3. Right-click the object to get to its contextual menu.

4. Choose Rotate Selection.

5. Click and drag the selection rectangle's corners to rotate the object (**Figure 9.9**).

Editing in Adobe Illustrator

Acrobat also lets you edit graphics in Adobe Illustrator. This ability opens up a vast array of editing possibilities. The cool part is that when you save the modified graphic in Illustrator, it's inserted back into the PDF file. I get excited about this feature! (Yes, I do lead a simple life.)

To edit artwork in Illustrator:

1. Click the TouchUp Object tool in the Advanced Editing toolbar.

2. Do either of the following:

▲ Hold down the Alt/Option key, and double-click the artwork.

▲ Right-click the object, and choose Edit Object from the contextual menu.

Acrobat launches Illustrator and opens the artwork in a new Illustrator window.

continues on next page

MODIFING LINE ART

3. Edit the artwork using usual Illustrator tools.

You may do anything that is valid in Illustrator, including adding new artwork or text. (The eyes and smile in **Figure 9.10** were added in Illustrator.)

4. In Illustrator, choose File > Save.

Illustrator saves the artwork directly into the original PDF file (**Figure 9.11**).

✔ Tip

■ The Acrobat Preferences allow you to use alternative editors, instead of Illustrator and Photoshop. Go to the Preferences dialog box, and choose the Touch Up category. You'll see a pair of controls that let you choose editing software for graphics and images.

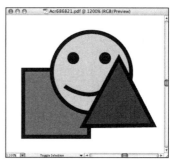

Figure 9.10 You can do anything you wish to PDF artwork you've opened in Illustrator; here we've added eyes and a smile to the circle.

Figure 9.11 When you save the artwork from Illustrator, the modified objects are inserted into the original PDF file.

Editing Images

The TouchUp Object tool works with images exactly as it does with line art. Right-clicking an image provides a contextual menu with the commands we discussed, which you use exactly the same way (**Figure 9.12**).

Option/Alt double-clicking an image opens that image in Adobe Photoshop, allowing you to perform any modification to that image that you wish. Saving the image from Photoshop inserts the modified image back into the original PDF file.

Figure 9.12 Right-clicking an image with the TouchUp Object tool yields a contextual menu that lets you move, rotate, and otherwise modify the image.

MODIFING LINE ART

Adding Headers and Footers

Acrobat allows you to add headers and footers to a PDF file. This new text can be in any font and point size, and can include page numbers and the current date.

The Add Header and Footer dialog box (**Figure 9.13**), although complex, isn't as confusing as it may seem at first.

Note that the header and footer each have three text fields, corresponding to left justified, centered, and right justified. You may supply up to three pieces of text for both the header and the footer, one snippet of text for each of the three positions.

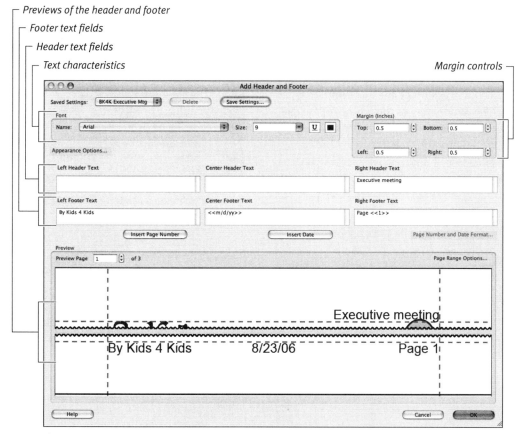

Figure 9.13 Here are the main sets of controls in the Add Header and Footer dialog box.

To add a header or footer to a document:

1. Choose Document > Header & Footer > Add.

   The Add Header and Footer dialog box opens (Figure 9.13).

2. Choose the font and size you want for your header and footer text.

   Note that controls to the right of the Size combo box let you turn on underlining and specify a text color.

3. In the Margin fields, type the values you want for the left, right, top, and bottom margins.

   The top margin is the baseline for the header; the footer is placed just below the bottom margin.

4. In the six text fields running across the center of the dialog box, type the left-justified, centered, and right-justified text for the header and/or footer.

   The preview across the bottom of the dialog box shows what your text will look like in place on your document page.

   Note that at any time while typing text, you can click the Insert Page Number or Insert Date button to insert the respective value into your text.

5. If you want your header and footer to apply only to certain pages in your document, click the Page Range Options link.

   Acrobat opens a dialog box that lets you specify the pages to which the header and footer should be applied (**Figure 9.14**).

6. Click OK.

   Acrobat adds the header and footer to your document (**Figure 9.15**).

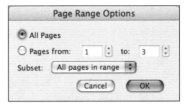

Figure 9.14 Clicking the Page Range Options link yields this dialog box, which lets you specify the pages to which your headers and footers should be applied.

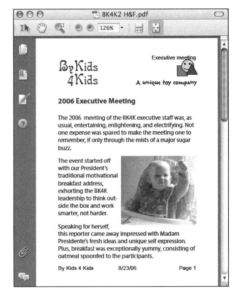

Figure 9.15 When you close the Add Header and Footer dialog box, your new text appears at the top and bottom of your PDF pages.

Figure 9.16 The Save Settings button lets you add the current set of control settings to the Saved Settings pop-up menu.

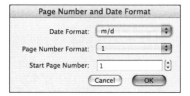

Figure 9.17 Clicking the Page Number and Date Format link lets you specify how the page numbers and date should appear on the page.

✔ Tips

■ If you have a header and footer combination that you use frequently, you can save your settings by clicking the Save Settings button in the Add Header and Footer dialog box (**Figure 9.16**). You're asked to name the collection of settings; that name will appear in the Saved Settings pop-up menu.

■ You can control the appearance of the page number and date inserted into your text. Click the Page Number and Date Format link to the right of the Insert Date button. Acrobat opens a dialog box that lets you select among a set of predefined formats (**Figure 9.17**).

■ You can modify your header and footer settings by selecting Document > Header & Footer > Update. The Add Header and Footer dialog box opens, filled in with your current settings. Make whatever changes you want, and click OK.

■ You can delete your header and footer by selecting Document > Header & Footer > Remove.

Adding a Background

Acrobat can add a background to the pages in your document. That background can be either a solid color or page contents taken from another PDF or image file. In the latter case, depending on the type of file you choose, the page contents can be any combination of text or graphics.

To add a background to your document pages:

1. Choose Document > Background > Add/ Replace.

   The Add Background dialog box opens (**Figure 9.18**).

2. If you want to use a page from another PDF file as your background, click the File radio button.

3. Click the Choose button, and select a file that you want to use as the source of your background.

4. In the Page Number field, specify the page within the file you want to use.

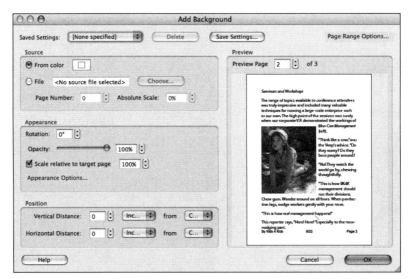

Figure 9.18 The Add Background dialog box lets you apply a background color or artwork to your PDF pages.

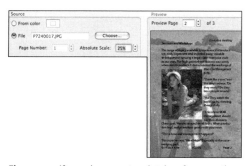

Figure 9.19 if you choose artwork taken from another PDF file, your background can be any combination of text, line art, and images.

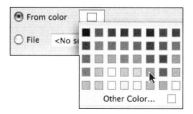

Figure 9.20 To apply a color as a background, choose the color from the color-well control.

5. In the Absolute Scale field, type the zoom you want to apply to the imported page.

   Note that the preview reflects your choice of background (**Figure 9.19**).

6. Choose an opacity for the background by either using the slider control or typing a percentage value into the text field.

   Reducing the opacity is important because it can keep the new background from overpowering the original page contents.

7. If you want your background to apply only to certain pages in your document, click the Page Range Options link, as described in the task "To add a header or footer to a document."

8. Click OK.

✔ Tips

- If you want a solid color for your background, click the "From color" radio button, and then click the color-well control and choose a color from the resulting color palette (**Figure 9.20**). The only control in the dialog box that has meaning is the Page Range Options link. The other settings apply only to imported PDF pages.

- You can save common background settings by clicking the Save Settings button. Acrobat lets you specify a name that will appear in the Saved Settings pop-up menu.

ADDING A BACKGROUND

Adding a Watermark

A *watermark* is text or graphics that are placed on a page either in front of or behind the page's contents. The watermark may be text, a logo, or other page contents taken from another PDF, Illustrator, or image file.

To add a watermark to a document's pages:

1. Choose Document > Watermark > Add. Acrobat will present you with the Add Watermark dialog box (**Figure 9.21**).

2. If you want a text watermark, click the Text radio button.

3. Type the text you want for your watermark.

4. Choose a font and size for the watermark text.

5. Click one of the alignment buttons.

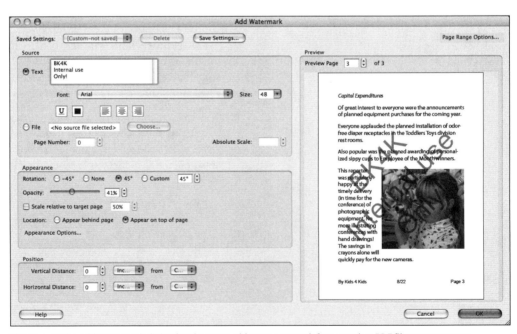

Figure 9.21 The Add Watermark dialog box lets you add text or artwork from another PDF file to your pages.

6. Choose an opacity for the watermark by either using the Opacity slider or typing a percentage into the text field.

It's important to reduce the watermark's opacity so that your original page contents remain readable.

7. Specify whether the watermark should be in front of or behind the page contents by clicking the appropriate Location radio button.

8. If you want your watermark to apply to only certain pages in your document, click the Page Range Options link, as described in the task "To add a header or footer to a document."

9. Click OK.

✔ Tip

■ If you want to use a page in another PDF file as your watermark, click the File radio button, and then follow the directions in the previous task for adding a background.

Redacting a Document

Acrobat Pro Only: *Redaction* refers to marking out or otherwise rendering unreadable sensitive parts of a document, usually to preserve information secrecy. This may be done to protect legal or trade secrets or to prevent the names and addresses of individuals from being broadcast.

In Acrobat, redaction is a three-step process. First you set the redaction properties, specifying how redacted items appear on the page. Next, you go through the document and choose the text and graphics that should be redacted. Finally, you apply redaction to the marked items. Acrobat replaces each redacted item with a colored block (a *redaction overlay*), optionally containing a text message (**Figure 9.22**).

Once redacted, the items are permanently unreadable; the process cannot be undone. (It wouldn't be worth much if it could be undone, now would it?)

Redaction is most conveniently carried out using the Redaction toolbar (**Figure 9.23**).

To set redaction properties:

1. In the Redaction toolbar, click Redaction Properties.

   The Redaction Tool Properties dialog box opens (**Figure 9.24**).

2. Choose the color you want for the redaction overlays by clicking in the color well and selecting a color from the resulting color picker.

3. If you want to have text placed into the redaction overlays, choose Use Overlay Text.

4. Choose your text characteristics: font, size, color, and alignment.

   Remember that the text color must be readable against the color you chose in step 2.

Figure 9.22 Redacted items in your PDF file are covered with opaque redaction overlays. (*Exp. Del.* Is short for *Expletive Deleted*, if you were curious.)

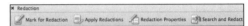

Figure 9.23 The Redaction toolbar has the tools you use to carry out redaction.

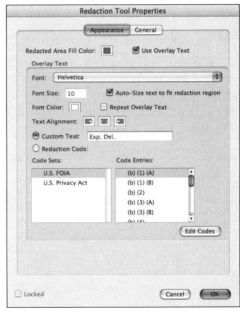

Figure 9.24 The Redaction Tool Properties dialog box let you specify the appearance of the redaction overlays.

Also popular was the planned awarding of personal-
ized sippy cups to Employee of the Month winners.

This reporter
was particularly
happy at the
timely delivery
(in time for the
conference) of
photographic
equipment. No
more illustrating
conferences with
hand drawings!
The savings in
crayons alone will

Figure 9.25 Items you've selected for redaction are outlined with a thick border.

Figure 9.26 When the Select for Redaction pointer moves over a redaction marker, the rectangle changes to show how the final redaction overlay will look.

5. If you want to supply your own text for the overlay, type the text into the Custom Text box.

6. If you want to use a standard code to indicate the reason for the redaction, choose one from among the code sets.

Acrobat provides codes for the U.S. Freedom of Information Act and the U.S. Privacy Act. You can add your own sets of codes, if you wish; consult the Acrobat 8 Help to see how to do this.

7. Click OK.

✔ **Tips**

■ I always click the "Auto-Size text to fit redaction region" check box. Acrobat picks a font size for each redacted item that makes the overlay text exactly fit the overlay.

■ Although you technically don't have to reset the redaction properties for each document you redact, I find I usually do, since I want a different label for the overlay.

To redact items in a document:

1. In the Redaction toolbar, click Mark for Redaction.

The mouse pointer turns into an I-beam when it's over text and a crosshairs when it's over white space in your document.

2. With the I-beam pointer, choose all the text that needs to be hidden.

3. With the crosshairs, drag enclosing rectangles around all artwork or other items that need to be obscured.

Acrobat draws a thick rectangle around the marked text and artwork (**Figure 9.25**). When the mouse pointer moves over it, the rectangle changes to show the redaction overlay that will be placed there when the redaction is applied (**Figure 9.26**).

continues on next page

REDACTING A DOCUMENT

4. In the Redaction toolbar, click the Apply Redaction button.

Acrobat hides all the redacted items with redaction overlays (Figure 9.22).

Acrobat then examines your document, looking for other internal information that you may also want to remove for security's sake. This includes comments, bookmarks, and electronic signatures. If Acrobat finds any of these items, the Examine Document dialog box opens (**Figure 9.27**).

5. Choose the check boxes corresponding to the items you want Acrobat to remove from your document.

6. Click "Remove all checked items."

Acrobat removes the internal objects and returns you to your now-redacted document page.

Acrobat marks the newly redacted document as Save-As Only. When you close the document, the standard Save dialog box opens, prompting you to save the document with a new name.

✔ Tip

- While you are marking items for redaction, you can change your mind and remove the mark from an item. To do so, click its marking rectangle, and press the Delete or Backspace key. You need to do this before you apply the redaction.

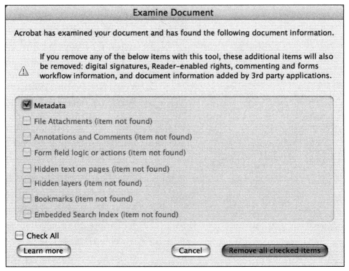

Figure 9.27 Having redacted the items you selected, Acrobat searches the document for other, hidden items you may want to remove.

Search and Redact

As a great convenience, Acrobat can search for words and phrases in your document's text and redact all instances of that text. The process is similar to searching for text, as discussed in Chapter 2.

To redact all instances of a phrase in a document:

1. In the Redaction toolbar, click Search and Redact.

   Acrobat opens the Search dialog box and zooms your document page out so the two windows (Search and Document) together fill your screen (**Figure 9.28**).

2. Type into the Search dialog box's text field the phrase or word you want to redact.

continues on next page

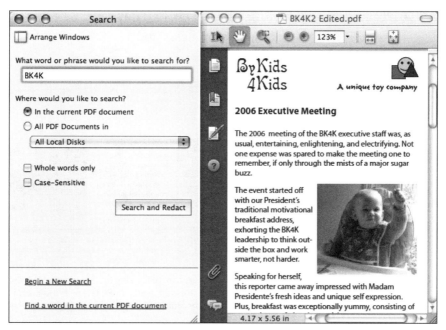

Figure 9.28 Clicking the Search and Redact tool lets you specify a word or phrase that should be redacted throughout your document.

3. Click the Search and Redact button.

The Search dialog box opens and presents you with a list of instances of the search phrase found in the document (**Figure 9.29**). Each item in this list has a check box next to it, indicating that that instance should be redacted.

4. Click the check boxes for all the instances in the list that you want to redact.

You can also click the Check All button to choose all items in the list.

5. Click the Mark Checked Results for Redaction button.

Acrobat marks for redaction all checked instances of the text in the document (**Figure 9.30**).

6. In the Redaction toolbar, click Apply Redaction.

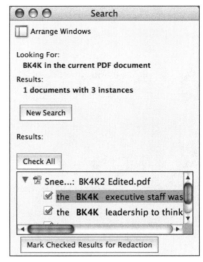

Figure 9.29 The Search window presents a list of all the instances of the found text. Clicking an item's check box marks the item for redaction.

Figure 9.30 Clicking the Search window's Mark Checked Results for Redaction button causes all the checkmarked items to be marked for redaction.

REDACTING A DOCUMENT

ADDING SIMPLE NAVIGATION FEATURES

10

If your PDF document is intended to be read onscreen, you'll make life much easier for your reader if you provide some minimal tools for navigating the document. The easiest—and most consistently useful—navigation tools you can add to your document are bookmarks, links, and articles. These are the topics of this chapter.

Adding Bookmarks to a Document

Bookmarks constitute a clickable table of contents that reside in the Bookmarks navigation pane (**Figure 10.1**). Clicking a bookmark takes you to the corresponding *view* within the document.

A *view* in Acrobat terminology is a combination of a page, a position on that page, and a zoom value (**Figure 10.2**).

To add a bookmark to a document, you set the document window to reflect the page, position, and zoom you want for that bookmark, and then you create the bookmark, which records that view as its destination.

To create a bookmark in a document:

1. Using the normal Acrobat navigation tools, set the document window to display the view you want as the bookmark's target.

2. Open the Bookmark pane by clicking the Bookmark icon.

3. Click the New Bookmark icon at the top of the bookmark list (**Figure 10.3**).

   Acrobat inserts a new bookmark named Untitled into the Bookmarks pane. The name is already selected so you can type over it.

4. Type the name you want for the new bookmark.

5. Click outside the Bookmarks pane or press Enter/Return to make the new name permanent.

✔ Tips

- Clicking a bookmark selects that bookmark in the list. New bookmarks are inserted into the list immediately after the currently selected bookmark.

Figure 10.1 Bookmarks make up a clickable table of contents that resides in the Bookmarks pane.

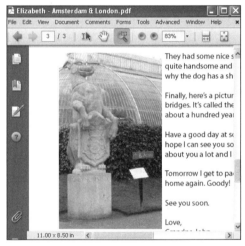

Figure 10.2 A bookmark's destination is a *view:* a combination of page, location on the page, and zoom level.

Figure 10.3 Clicking the New Bookmark icon creates a new bookmark named Untitled.

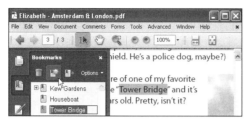

Figure 10.4 If you select text and then create a new bookmark, the selected text becomes the bookmark's title.

Figure 10.5 You can drag a bookmark to a new location in the Bookmarks list.

Figure 10.6 The Bookmark Properties dialog box lets you change the style and color of your bookmark's text in the list.

- If you select text on your document page with the Select tool (**Figure 10.4**) and then create a bookmark, the selected text is used as the new bookmark's name.

- You can easily rearrange bookmarks by dragging them to their new location in the list. A bit less obvious is the fact that you can drag a bookmark to be a descendent of another (**Figure 10.5**). Once child bookmarks have been moved into another bookmark, you can display or hide them using the disclosure control to the left of the parent bookmark; this control is a plus sign in Windows and a triangle on the Macintosh, as usual.

- You can select and move multiple bookmarks at one time. To do so, hold down the Command/Control key to select individual bookmarks or the Shift key to select a contiguous range of bookmarks in the list.

You can make a bookmark stand out in the list by changing its color or its text style.

To change a bookmark's color and text style:

1. Open the Bookmarks pane, if necessary.

2. Right-click the bookmark whose properties you want to change.

3. In the resulting contextual menu, choose Properties.

   The Bookmark Properties dialog box opens (**Figure 10.6**).

4. Choose a text style from the drop-down menu.

   You can choose from among the standard styles: bold, italic, and bold-italic.

continues on next page

ADDING BOOKMARKS TO A DOCUMENT

5. Click the color well, and choose a color from the resulting palette.

6. Click OK.

✔ Tip

■ I often use style to accentuate a document's structure. Bolding the bookmarks associated with chapter titles makes them stand out well; in some documents, I'll make the bookmarks of the very important topics red.

Sometimes you need to change the destination of a bookmark, often because you have changed the document—inserted new pages, perhaps—and the new contents are a better destination for the bookmark. Changing the bookmark's target is very easy to do.

To change an existing bookmark's destination:

1. Using the standard Acrobat navigation and zoom tools, set the document window so it displays the new destination you want for the bookmark.

2. Open the Bookmarks pane, if necessary.

3. Right-click the bookmark whose destination you want to change.

4. Choose Set Destination in the contextual menu.

Acrobat opens a dialog box asking if you're sure you want to change the bookmark's destination (**Figure 10.7**).

5. Click Yes.

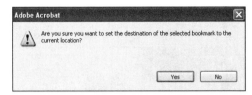

Figure 10.7 When you change the destination of a bookmark, Acrobat gives you a chance to change your mind.

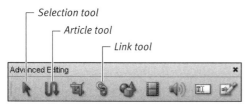

Figure 10.8 The Advanced Editing toolbar contains three tools you use in this chapter

Figure 10.9 The Create Link dialog box lets you specify the appearance and behavior of a link.

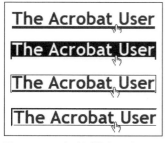

Figure 10.10 The highlight style specifies how a link changes when you click it. From top to bottom, they are None (boring), Invert, Outline, and Inset.

Creating Links

Links are the easiest way to make a PDF file a dynamic online document. They are, in effect, bookmarks that reside on your document page, rather than in a navigation pane. They behave exactly like the links familiar to you on Web sites: You click the "hot" area of the link, and something happens; usually, the link sends you to another view in the document.

Links can have a visible border, but otherwise no icons or labels are associated with them. If you want such artwork, it must already be part of the contents of the PDF page; you lay the link on top of the existing graphics or text on the page.

You create links with the Link tool in the Advanced Editing toolbar (**Figure 10.8**).

To create a link on a page:

1. In the Advanced Editing toolbar, click the Link tool.

   The mouse pointer changes to a crosshairs.

2. Click and drag a rectangle on the PDF page where you want the link to be.

   Acrobat displays the Create Link dialog box (**Figure 10.9**).

3. Using the standard navigation and zoom tools, set the view in the document window to the destination of the new link.

4. If you want a visible rectangle around the link, choose Visible Rectangle in the Link Type drop-down menu; otherwise, choose Invisible Rectangle.

5. If you chose a visible rectangle for your link, specify the thickness, style, and color you want for the rectangle.

6. Choose a highlight style for the link (**Figure 10.10**).

continues on next page

CREATING LINKS

7. In the Link Action radio buttons, choose "Go to a page view."

See the sidebar "Link Actions" for a discussion of the other actions.

8. Click Next.

The Create Go to View dialog box opens (**Figure 10.11**). This dialog box behaves like a palette, in that your Acrobat document is still active in the background; the navigation and zoom tools still function to move you around in the document.

9. Use the navigation and zoom tools to set the document view to the link's destination.

10. Click Set Link.

Acrobat returns your document window to the link's page. Your new link is visible as a bounding rectangle (**Figure 10.12**); when the mouse pointer rolls over this rectangle, handles appear at its sides and corners, as in the figure.

11. Adjust the position of the link by dragging its bounding rectangle.

12. Adjust the size of the link by dragging the handles at the sides and corners of its bounding rectangle.

13. To make another link, repeat steps 2–12.

14. When you're finished making links, click the Acrobat Hand tool.

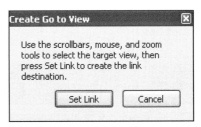

Figure 10.11 While the Create Go to View dialog box is open, the document window is active in the background; you can use the arrow keys and other navigation tools to move around the document.

Figure 10.12 A link can be resized and repositioned by dragging the bounding rectangle or its handles with the Link tool.

Link Actions

The Create Link dialog box (Figure 10.9) has four radio buttons you can choose among to specify what your link should do. The default action is "Go to a page view," which displays a new view in the document window when you click the link.

The other three radio buttons have the following meanings:

◆ **Open a file** creates a link that opens a spreadsheet, word-processing, or other file on your computer. Clicking the finished link opens the file in whatever application is associated with that type of file.

When you click the Next button in the Create Link dialog box, Acrobat lets you specify the file to be opened.

◆ **Open a web page** tells the link to launch your default Web browser with a particular Web page. When you click the dialog box's Next button, Acrobat opens a

dialog box into which you can type the URL of the Web page (**Figure 10.13**).

◆ **Custom link** provides access to more than a dozen advanced actions available to a link. Clicking Next takes you to the Actions Tab in the Link Properties dialog box (**Figure 10.14**), whose Select Action menu lets you choose the action you want. This can be anything from playing a sound to executing an Acrobat menu item.

We'll talk about some of these actions in the next chapter. However, most of them are beyond the scope of this book. See the Acrobat Help files for more information.

Interestingly, the advanced actions are also available to your bookmarks. If you right-click a bookmark and choose Properties from the contextual menu, you get a dialog box with the same Actions tab shown in Figure 10.14.

Figure 10.13 The Edit URL dialog box lets you specify a Web address to associate with a link.

Figure 10.14 The Actions tab of the Link Properties dialog box lets you assign one of a variety of advanced actions to a link.

Modifying Existing Links

Whenever the Link tool is selected, all the links in your document appear as black bounding rectangles on the page. Clicking one of these rectangles selects that link; the bounding rectangle changes color, and handles appear whenever the mouse pointer moves over the rectangle (Figure 10.12).

You can make a number of changes to a link when it's selected with the Link tool.

To modify an existing link:

1. Click the Link tool in the Advanced Editing toolbar.

2. Click the link you want to modify.

3. To change the position of the link, drag its bounding rectangle to the new location.

4. To change the size of the link, drag the handles at the sides and corners of the rectangle.

5. To change the appearance of the link, right-click the link and choose Properties from the contextual menu.

    Acrobat displays the Appearance controls of the Link Properties dialog box (**Figure 10.15**), allowing you to reset the visibility, thickness, color, and other visual properties of the link.

6. To delete the link, press the Delete key. On Macintosh laptops, you need to hold the fn key and press the Delete key.

✔ Tips

- You can change multiple links at one time. To do so, hold down the Shift or Command/Ctrl key, and click the links you want to modify. Any changes you make apply to all the selected links.

Figure 10.15 The Appearance tab of the Link Properties dialog box lets you specify the visual characteristics of a link.

- You can nudge the position and size of a selected link. Pressing an arrow key moves the selected link one pixel in the corresponding direction. Holding down the Shift key and pressing an arrow key increases or decreases the size of the link by one pixel.

- You can delete all the links in your document by selecting Advanced > Document Processing > Remove All Links. Acrobat lets you select the pages from which to remove all the links.

- You can also double-click a link with the Link tool to obtain the Link Properties dialog box (Figure 10.15).

Figure 10.16 The Create Web Links dialog box lets you specify the pages that should be searched for URLs.

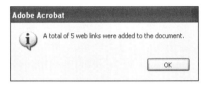

Figure 10.17 Acrobat tells you how many Web links it added to your file.

Making Automatic Web Links

The "Link Actions" sidebar discusses making a link to a Web page; when the reader clicks on this link, Acrobat launches the default Web browser and opens the Web page tied to that link. Acrobat sensibly refers to such links as *Web links*.

Acrobat can automatically make Web links throughout your document. The Create Web Links command searches the text in your PDF file and places links over any Web or email addresses it finds. Web addresses in the text receive links to that URL; email addresses get links that open the default mail client with a blank message addressed to the target email address.

To add Web links to your document:

1. With the document open to any page, choose Advanced > Document Processing > Create Links from URLs.

   Acrobat will present you with the Create Web Links dialog box (**Figure 10.16**).

2. Enter the beginning and ending page numbers of the range that should be scanned for URLs, or click All to select all pages.

3. Click OK.

   Acrobat scans your PDF file, adding links to all the URLs it finds. When it's finished, Acrobat reports on the number of links it added (**Figure 10.17**).

MAKING AUTOMATIC WEB LINKS

Creating Articles

An *article* is a set of rectangular regions scattered throughout your document that, taken together, represent a single thread of text. It's similar to an article in a newspaper, which may start on the front page, continue on pages 13 and 14, and finish up on page 27.

Articles are extremely useful for taking documents that were originally laid out for print—usually with small point sizes, often with multiple columns—and making them readable online. I've used articles a lot in my documents and tend to get unreasonably enthusiastic about them!

When your mouse pointer moves over an article on a page, the pointer turns into a hand with a downward-pointing arrow (**Figure 10.18**). When you click the article, Acrobat zooms in until the article exactly fits across the width of the document window (**Figure 10.19**). This makes the text easy to read.

Figure 10.18 When the mouse pointer moves over an article, it turns into a hand with a downward arrow.

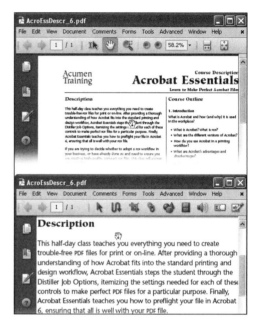

Figure 10.19 When you click an article (top), Acrobat zooms in until the article fills the width of the document window (bottom).

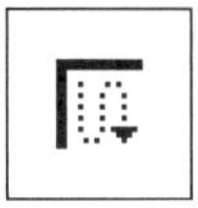

Figure 10.20 When you click the Article tool, the mouse pointer becomes a wavy arrow.

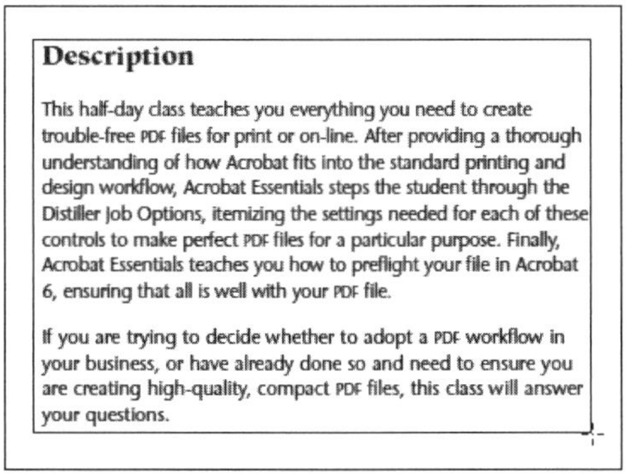

Description

This half-day class teaches you everything you need to create trouble-free PDF files for print or on-line. After providing a thorough understanding of how Acrobat fits into the standard printing and design workflow, Acrobat Essentials steps the student through the Distiller Job Options, itemizing the settings needed for each of these controls to make perfect PDF files for a particular purpose. Finally, Acrobat Essentials teaches you how to preflight your file in Acrobat 6, ensuring that all is well with your PDF file.

If you are trying to decide whether to adopt a PDF workflow in your business, or have already done so and need to ensure you are creating high-quality, compact PDF files, this class will answer your questions.

Figure 10.21 With the Article tool, you drag out a series of rectangles that will be the sections of your article text.

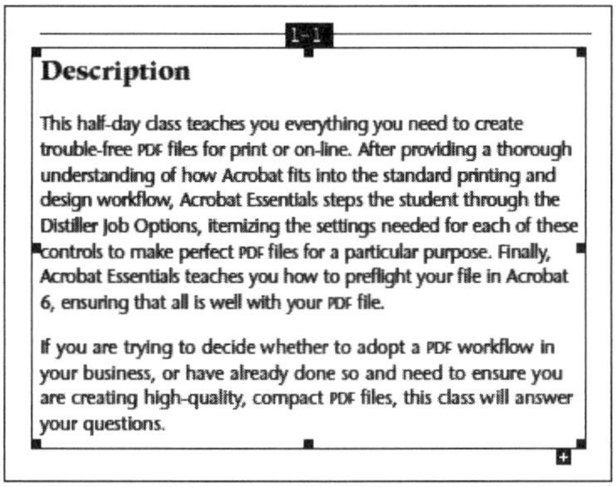

1-1

Description

This half-day class teaches you everything you need to create trouble-free PDF files for print or on-line. After providing a thorough understanding of how Acrobat fits into the standard printing and design workflow, Acrobat Essentials steps the student through the Distiller Job Options, itemizing the settings needed for each of these controls to make perfect PDF files for a particular purpose. Finally, Acrobat Essentials teaches you how to preflight your file in Acrobat 6, ensuring that all is well with your PDF file.

If you are trying to decide whether to adopt a PDF workflow in your business, or have already done so and need to ensure you are creating high-quality, compact PDF files, this class will answer your questions.

Figure 10.22 Each section of your article is identified by an article number and a section number within that article.

While you're reading an article, each click of the mouse button takes you down one screen within the article, changing from one column to another as needed. No scrolling, dragging, or fussing with navigation buttons is required.

When you reach the end of the article, a final click reverts the view to what it was before you entered the article.

To create an article in a document:

1. In the Advanced Editing toolbar, click the Article tool.

   The mouse pointer turns into the wavy arrow shape (**Figure 10.20**).

2. Click-and-drag a rectangle, indicating the first area in the article (**Figure 10.21**).

   While you're dragging out the rectangle, the mouse pointer is a crosshair.

3. Continue to click and drag additional rectangles in the order that a reader should see them.

   When you are finished, each of your article segments is surrounded by a black rectangle labeled with an article number and a segment number (**Figure 10.22**). Note that if you click a segment with the Article tool, Acrobat provides you with the handles visible in Figure 10.22, which allow you to resize the article.

continues on next page

CREATING ARTICLES

4. When you've dragged out all the article segments, click the Article tool again (or any other tool, for that matter) to indicate you're finished constructing your article.

Acrobat will present you with the Article Properties dialog box (**Figure 10.23**). The information this dialog box requests is all optional, but it will make your article more useful to the reader.

5. Type in some combination of title, subject, author, and searchable keywords.

6. Click OK.

You've now created your article, which will behave properly as soon as you click the Hand tool.

✔ Tip

■ Acrobat has an Article navigation pane (hidden by default) that lists all the articles in the current document. You can make pane this visible, as usual, by choosing View > Navigation Panels > Articles.

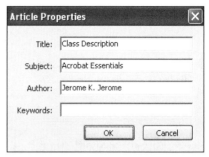

Figure 10.23 When you've defined all of the sections of your article, you can specify a title, subject, author, and searchable keywords for the article.

CREATING AN ACROBAT PRESENTATION

Acrobat provides a range of features that makes it easy to use a PDF document as a presentation for a variety of situations:

◆ Group presentations, in which you're displaying the PDF pages using a computer projector. In this case, the PDF file replaces the more common (though not as graphically sophisticated) PowerPoint file.

◆ Distributed presentation files that are intended to be viewed by readers on their own computers. This may be an electronic brochure, distributed on the Web.

◆ Kiosk presentations, in which the PDF document is viewed in a public place on a dedicated computer. A "Where to Go" kiosk in an airport is a good example.

PDF documents can be viewed full-screen with all the transitions and navigational control offered by any other presentation software. Furthermore, graphic and typographic control in Acrobat documents is much better than in other presentation software.

This chapter covers the features that allow you to turn an Acrobat document into a presentation file.

Setting Open Options

In a presentation, the Acrobat toolbars and navigation panes are a distraction. You want readers to see only your document and just enough of an interface to let them move around in the document.

Acrobat gives you the ability to control what should be displayed when a document is opened. These *open options* are stored with the document, so whenever readers open that document, you control exactly what they see.

To set a document's open options:

1. Choose File > Properties.

   The Document Properties dialog box opens.

2. Click the Initial View tab to see the controls that determine how the document will be presented to the user (**Figure 11.1**).

3. In the "Navigation tab" pop-up menu, choose Page Only.

   This option specifies that all the navigation panes should be hidden.

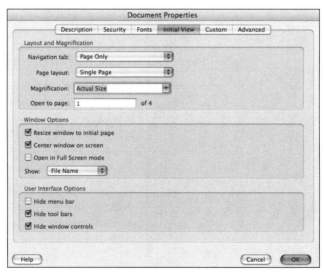

Figure 11.1 The Initial View pane in the Document Properties dialog box lets you specify what readers see when they first opening your document.

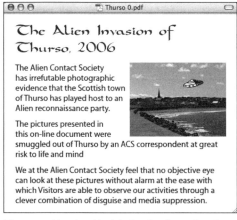

Figure 11.2 You should minimize the distractions in an Acrobat presentation by hiding the toolbars and other user interface elements.

4. In the "Page layout" pop-up menu, choose Single Page.

The alternatives, which display multiple pages side-by-side or vertically, aren't good for a presentation.

5. In the Magnification pop-up menu, choose Actual Size.

6. Choose the "Resize window to initial page" check box.

The document will open in a window that exactly matches the page size. There won't be a gray border around the page in the document window.

7. Choose "Center window on screen."

8. If you want your presentation to take over the entire computer screen, choose the "Open in Full Screen mode" check box.

9. Choose "Hide tool bars."

The toolbars are distracting in a presentation.

10. Choose "Hide window controls."

This option hides the navigation pane icons, which are also distracting during a presentation.

Steps 9 and 10 leave your document window displaying only page content, as in **Figure 11.2**.

✔ Tip

- Full Screen mode is useful for corporate presentations or for kiosk documents. I recommend against it if you'll be distributing your PDF document to other readers; most people find it annoying when a document covers everything else on their computers. We'll talk more about Full Screen documents in the next section.

Creating a Full Screen Slide Show

If you're using a PDF file for a group presentation, you will often want Acrobat to display your document as a full-screen display, masking all user-interface items. This eliminates distractions and makes the document's contents large and legible. In effect, you're presenting a slide show to your audience.

If your document will only be used full-screen, then you can set its Initial View properties to automatically display the document full screen, as described in the previous section.

On the other hand, if this document is one you use in a variety of circumstances—or you just don't like having full-screen display invoked automatically—then you should turn on Full Screen mode only as needed.

To turn on Full Screen mode:

◆ With the document open, choose View > Full Screen Mode (**Figure 11.3**).

Acrobat displays your document zoomed so it fills the entire screen.

To exit Full Screen mode:

◆ Press the Escape key.

Acrobat returns you to viewing the document in a window.

Moving around in Full Screen mode

Full Screen mode hides the entire Acrobat user interface, leaving you no buttons or other visual controls you can use to navigate through the document. How do you move through your full-screen presentation?

In fact, there are several ways you can navigate a full-screen document:

◆ To move to the next page, click anywhere on the screen or press the Right Arrow or Down key.

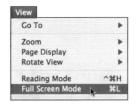

Figure 11.3 You can manually open a document in Full Screen mode from the View menu.

Figure 11.4 The Set Transitions dialog box lets you apply special effects that are used when you move from one page to another in your Full Screen document.

Figure 11.5 You can choose from among a variety of transitions built into Acrobat.

◆ To move to the previous page, Shift-click anywhere on the page, right-click anywhere on the page, or press the Left Arrow or Up key.

◆ To go to the beginning of the document, press the Home key.

◆ To go to the end of the document, press the End key.

Adding transitions

Acrobat supplies a number of transition effects you can use when moving from one page to another in Full Screen mode. These have name evocative of what they look like, such as Dissolve, Fade, and Split. They're next to impossible to describe, so I recommend you experiment with them to see what they do.

To specify a transition for Full Screen mode:

1. With your document open, choose Advanced > Document Processing > Page Transitions.

   Acrobat displays the Set Transitions dialog box (**Figure 11.4**).

2. Select the transition you want from the Transition pop-up menu (**Figure 11.5**).

3. Select a direction (horizontal or vertical) for the transition, if appropriate.

   Not all transitions have a direction.

4. Choose a transition speed (slow, medium, or fast) from the Speed pop-up menu.

5. If you want the document to turn the page automatically, then choose Auto Flip and specify a duration.

6. Use the Page Range controls to choose the pages to which the transition should apply.

7. Click OK.

Keep in mind that these settings do not affect viewing the document unless you're in Full Screen mode.

CREATING A FULL SCREEN SLIDE SHOW

Creating a Next Page Button

Acrobat provides a variety of keys and clicks that let you go from one page to the next in Full Screen mode. However, most people find it comforting to have visible controls to navigate within the document (**Figure 11.6**). Here you'll see how to add Next Page and Previous Page buttons to your document.

The easiest way to create a Next Page button is to make the button artwork part of the original page design, as in Figure 11.6, and then lay on top of the button a link that does the work.

The following task steps through the creation of a Next Page button. You can use nearly the same steps to create a Previous Page button.

These steps assume the button artwork is already on the page.

To create a Next Page button:

1. Click the Link tool in the Advanced Editing toolbar.

2. Click and drag a link rectangle around the Next Page button's artwork.

   The Create Link dialog box opens.

3. Choose the following settings:
   ▲ For Link Type, choose Invisible Rectangle.
   ▲ For Highlight Style, choose Inset.
   ▲ For Link Action, choose Custom link (**Figure 11.7**).

4. Click Next.

   The Link Properties dialog box opens.

5. Click the Actions tab (**Figure 11.8**).

6. In the Select Action pop-up menu, choose "Execute a menu item."

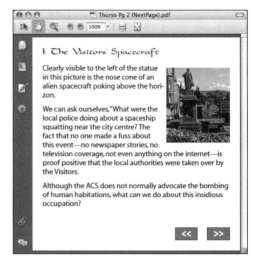

Figure 11.6 If a document is intended to be read in Full Screen mode, you should provide buttons that the reader can use to move within the document.

Figure 11.7 A Next Page button needs Custom Link as its action.

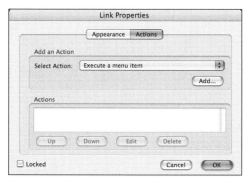

Figure 11.8 The Link Action for a Next Page button is "Execute a menu item."

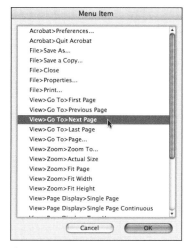

Figure 11.9 The menu item your link should execute is View > Go To > Next Page.

Figure 11.10 When you return to the Link Properties dialog box, the menu item appears in the Actions list.

Figure 11.11 With the Link tool still active, a rectangle surrounds the link that lets you position and resize the link so it fits the button artwork.

7. Click Add.

The Menu Item dialog box opens. This dialog box lists all the menu items in all of Acrobat's menus.

8. From the list in the Menu Item dialog box, choose View > Go To > Next Page (**Figure 11.9**).

For a Previous Page button, you would choose View > Go To > Previous Page.

9. Click OK.

Acrobat returns to the Link Properties dialog box, now showing your chosen menu item in its list of Actions (**Figure 11.10**).

10. Click OK.

Acrobat returns you to your document page. The Next Page artwork is now surrounded by a link's red border rectangle and handles, as in **Figure 11.11**.

11. Reposition and resize the link as necessary by dragging the rectangle and its handles.

12. Click the Hand tool (or any other tool) to indicate that you're finished creating the link.

When you click the Next Page button, Acrobat moves the document view to the next page.

✔ Tip

■ You can easily reproduce the Next Page link by copying it and then pasting it on other pages. Select the link with the Link tool, and then choose Edit > Copy (or use whatever technique you prefer to do a copy). Now, go to each page that has a Next Page button and paste the link onto the page.

CREATING A NEXT PAGE BUTTON

Creating a Self-Running Presentation

Acrobat lets you turn your document into a self-running slide show that moves from page to page without human intervention. This is extremely useful in retail situations, where a computer can run a presentation for passers-by to watch.

To turn a file into a self-running presentation, you must do two things, both of which apply to Full Screen mode: auto-flip the pages, so the document automatically moves from one page to the next; and tell Acrobat to loop the last page back to the first, so that the document plays itself indefinitely.

To create a self-running presentation:

1. Choose Advanced > Document Processing > Page Transitions.

   Acrobat displays the Set Transitions dialog box (Figure 11.4).

2. Choose Auto Flip, and specify a duration.

   Each page will be visible for the number of seconds specified.

3. Set the other Page Transition controls as described in the task "To specify a transition for Full Screen mode."

4. Click OK.

5. Choose Edit > Preferences in Windows or Acrobat 8 > Preferences on the Mac.

   The Preferences dialog box opens.

6. Choose Full Page in the Categories list.

   Acrobat displays Full Screen controls.

7. In the Full Screen Navigation section, choose "Loop after last page" (**Figure 11.12**).

   All your full-screen documents will wrap from the last page to the first. Unfortunately, there is no way to set this option for just a single document.

8. Click OK.

This document will always play as a self-running presentation when you put it into Full Screen mode.

✔ Tips

■ If you want the current document to always act as a full-screen presentation, remember that the Document Properties dialog box (Figure 11.1) has an "Open in Full Screen mode" check box among its Initial View options.

■ Note that the Preferences dialog box also allows you to specify a transition and auto-flip. If you select these as preferences, then every time you enter Full Screen mode, Acrobat applies the transition and automatically flips the page. I recommend against this unless you are creating a kiosk or have another situation in which you always want the same transition and the same auto-flip setting.

CREATING A SELF-RUNNING PRESENTATION

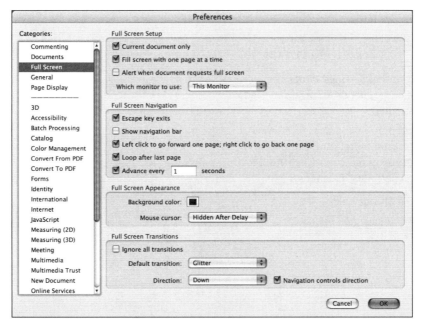

Figure 11.12 About halfway down the set of check boxes in the Full Screen controls is "Loop after last page," which is important for self-running presentations.

Placing a Movie on a Page

Acrobat Pro Only: Multimedia is becoming increasingly common in presentations. Marketing presentations and stand-alone kiosk displays often feature an animated walk-through or demonstration of a product.

Acrobat supports this marketing need by letting you place movies on your PDF pages. On the Macintosh, this can be any movie playable with QuickTime, including MPEG and most AVI files; in Windows, this can be any movie playable with QuickTime, Windows Media Player, RealPlayer, or Flash.

To place a movie on a PDF page:

1. Click the Movie tool in the Advanced Editing toolbar (**Figure 11.13**).

   The mouse pointer turns into a crosshair.

2. Click and drag a rectangle on the page where you want the movie to go.

   The size of the rectangle doesn't matter, since Acrobat will resize it to match the movie's native size.

   Acrobat will present you with the Add Movie dialog box (**Figure 11.14**).

3. In the Content Settings, choose between Acrobat 6 and later or Acrobat 5 and earlier compatibility.

   I suggest Acrobat 6 unless you have a strong reason for retaining compatibility with old copies of Acrobat. See the "Movie File Compatibility" sidebar.

4. Click the Choose button.

   The Open dialog box opens.

Figure 11.13 You place movies on a PDF page with the Movie tool in the Advanced Editing toolbar.

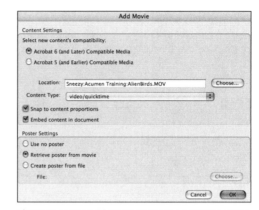

Figure 11.14 The Add Movie dialog box lets you specify the details of the movie you want to place on the page.

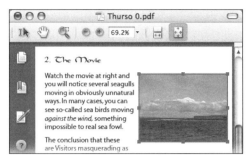

Figure 11.15 Your newly placed movie is surrounded by a rectangle that lets you reposition and resize it.

5. Select the movie file you want to place on the PDF page, and click OK.

6. Choose "Embed content in document."

   This is the safest choice, but see the sidebar "To Embed or Not to Embed" for a discussion of why you want to embed your movie (or not).

   The other settings in this dialog box default to reasonable values and should usually be left alone.

7. Click OK.

   Acrobat places the movie on the page. The placed movie is surrounded by a red rectangle with handles at its sides and corners (**Figure 11.15**). The picture showing in the rectangle is the movie's first frame.

   The rectangle and handles remain visible while the Movie tool is selected. You can get them back at any time later by clicking the movie with the Movie tool.

8. Drag the movie to its correct place on the page, and resize it by dragging the handles.

   You can retain the rectangle's original proportions when resizing it by holding down the Shift key as you drag its handles.

continues on next page

Movie File Compatibility

There are two types of compatibility to which you need to pay attention when placing a movie on a PDF page:

Acrobat 5 compatibility. Adobe added a great deal of movie capability with Acrobat 6. Acrobat 5 could play only QuickTime-compatible movies, even in Windows. Acrobat 6 and later give you Windows support for the additional file types.

Cross-platform compatibility. The only movie formats that work on both Mac and Windows are those that are playable with QuickTime.

9. To add a border around the movie, right-click the movie with the Movie tool and choose Properties from the contextual menu.

The Multimedia Properties dialog box opens. Its Appearance tab lets you specify the thickness and color of the border (**Figure 11.16**).

10. Click the Hand tool to finish placing the movie.

✔ Tip

■ The picture visible on the page when the movie isn't playing is called its *poster*. The default poster is the movie's first frame. Some movie files have a poster picture embedded in them, which Acrobat can use. If you wish, you can also choose "Create poster from file" in the Add Movie dialog box, click Choose, and pick a JPEG or other image file to use as the poster.

Figure 11.16 The Multimedia Properties dialog box lets you specify the thickness, style, and color of a rectangular border around your movie.

To Embed or Not to Embed

One of the choices you make in the Add Movie dialog box (Figure 11.14) is whether to embed the movie in the PDF document.

Generally, you should embed placed movies in your PDF file. Doing so makes the PDF file self-contained—you never have to worry about the movie getting lost.

There are two problems with embedding the movie: The PDF file becomes larger—potentially much larger—which puts a strain on bandwidth and storage. More important, an embedded movie requires Acrobat 6 or later to play; it can't be viewed by people with older versions of Acrobat.

If you don't embed the movie, it can be played by all versions of Acrobat. However, the movie data remains in the separate movie file, which must be available to Acrobat when the movie is played. When you move the PDF file to another disk or server, the movie file must travel with it. Furthermore, the movie must remain in the same location, relative to the PDF file; if the movie file was originally in the same folder as the PDF file, it must remain in the PDF file's folder when you move them both.

Figure 11.17 It's often easiest to have your button artwork as part of the page design and then lay links on top of it.

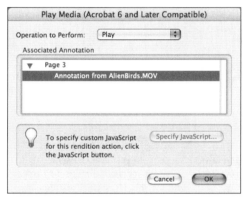

Figure 11.18 A link's Play Media action let you specify an action (Play, Pause, and so on) to perform on one of the movies in your document.

Figure 11.19 The Operation to Perform pop-up menu lets you choose from all the actions you can reasonably apply to a movie.

Playing a Movie

Once a movie has been placed, you can play it by clicking it with the Hand tool. Of course, it's nice to give the reader some visible Play/Pause/Stop controls. That's easily done with links.

The easiest way to create a Play Movie button is to place the button artwork on the page in the original document design (**Figure 11.17**). You can then lay links on top of the button graphic to do the actual work.

The following task steps through the creation of a Play button. Making buttons for Stop, Pause, and other commands is done virtually the same way. The steps presume the Play button's artwork is already on the PDF page.

To create a Play button:

1. Follow steps 1–5 in the task "To create a Next Page button."

2. In the Select Action pop-up menu of the Link Properties dialog box, choose either Play Media (Acrobat 6 Compatible) or Play Media (Acrobat 5 Compatible), according to the way you placed your movie (Figure 11.14).

3. Click Add.

    Acrobat will present you with the Play Media dialog box (**Figure 11.18**).

4. In the Operation to Perform pop-up menu, choose Play.

    Note that this pop-up menu has all the other actions you might perform with a movie: Pause, Stop, and so on (**Figure 11.19**).

5. The list in the Play Media dialog box contains all the movies placed in the document; in this list, click the movie you want to play.

continues on next page

PLAYING A MOVIE

6. Click OK.

Acrobat returns you to the Link Properties dialog box, which now lists Play Media in its Actions list (**Figure 11.20**).

7. Click OK.

Acrobat returns you to your page, which now has a link rectangle with handles that you can use to reposition and resize the link, as needed (**Figure 11.21**).

8. Click the Hand tool to finalize the link.

When you click the Play button, Acrobat plays the movie.

In some cases, you might want the movie to automatically play when the reader opens its page. You do this by creating a Page Action that Acrobat will carry out when the reader enters a particular page. Our page action will play our movie.

To automatically play a movie when a page opens:

1. With your document open, display the Pages navigation pane by clicking the Pages icon.

2. Right-click the thumbnail of the page that has your movie.

3. Choose Page Properties from the contextual menu (**Figure 11.22**).

The Page Properties dialog box opens.

4. Click the Actions tab.

5. In the Select Trigger pop-up menu, choose Page Open (**Figure 11.23**).

This option tells Acrobat to play the movie when the reader opens the page, rather than when the reader closes it.

6. Follow steps 2–8 in the task "To create a Play button," but assign the Play Media action.

Acrobat will now play the movie every time the page is opened.

Figure 11.20 When you return to the Link Properties dialog box, the Actions list includes your new Play Media action.

Figure 11.21 Your Play button is initially surrounded by the link's bounding rectangle, letting you reposition and resize the link.

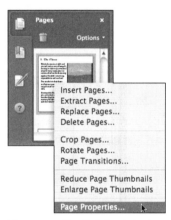

Figure 11.22 The first step in having a movie automatically play when the page opens is to access the Page Properties from the Pages navigation pane.

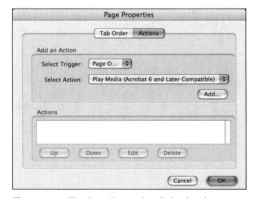

Figure 11.23 The Page Properties dialog box has an Actions pane virtually identical to that for links.

PLAYING A MOVIE

Figure 11.24 You place a multimedia sound on the page with the Sound tool in the Advanced Editing toolbar.

Adding Sound to a PDF Page

Acrobat Pro Only: The movie file formats supported by Acrobat might contain only a soundtrack, making them, in effect, sound files. You can place these sound files on the page like any other movie.

The Sound tool (**Figure 11.24**) in the Advanced Editing toolbar lets you attach a sound to a page in your PDF file. The steps are identical to embedding a movie, except you start with the Sound tool rather than the Movie tool.

To place a sound on a document page:

1. Click the Sound tool in the Advanced Editing toolbar.

2. Click and drag a rectangle on the page.

    The location of this rectangle is usually irrelevant, because most sounds have no visible marker.

    The Add Sound dialog box opens (**Figure 11.25**).

continues on next page

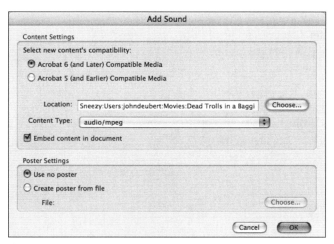

Figure 11.25 The Add Sound dialog box is virtually identical to the Add Movie dialog box, and you should use the same settings.

3. Follow the steps in the task "To place a movie on a PDF page."

You can place on the page any sound playable by QuickTime (including AIFF and MOV) and, in Windows, sounds playable by Windows Media Player, RealPlayer, and Flash.

When you're finished, your sound is on the page, but no visible cue indicates that it is there. (Unlike videos, there is no first frame that Acrobat can use as a poster on the page.) You should provide a Play button on the page so a reader can play the sound. You do this the same way you made the Play button for your placed movie.

✔ Tips

- Although sounds don't automatically get a poster, you can provide a picture to use as a marker on the page. In the Add Sound dialog box, choose "Create poster from file," and select a TIF, JPEG, or other picture file to use as a poster.

- As with videos, you can have Acrobat automatically play a sound (a bugle fanfare, perhaps) when the user opens the page. Follow the earlier directions for attaching a movie to a page, but choose a sound-only file as your movie.

- Use automatic sounds with restraint. A sound that plays every single time a reader passes through a page can get really annoying after the first hundred repetitions.

ADDING SOUND TO A PDF PAGE

ORGANIZING DOCUMENTS

One underused feature that Acrobat 8 inherited from Acrobat 7 is the Organizer. This astonishingly handy tool provides lists of your PDF files categorized a variety of ways for convenient access:

◆ You can find files according to when you last looked at them (yesterday, last week, and so on).

◆ You can find files in any location on your hard disk.

◆ You can create a list of favorite folders on your hard disk, which can be examined with a single click.

◆ You can create collections of PDF files pertaining to a particular task or topic. A collection's files can be scattered throughout your hard disk but are all accessible in the same list.

I find I use this tool all the time, particularly when I'm working on a project that requires repeated reference to a number of PDF-format reference documents.

Examining the Organizer

Opening the Organizer involves a single menu selection: File > Organizer > Open Organizer. As a shortcut, you can press Shift-Command/Control-1. You're now looking at the Organizer window (**Figure 12.1**).

This window has three columns. From left to right, these are as follows:

Places. This column has three panes, presenting collections of PDF files. Some of these collections are created for you, such as the collection of all files viewed yesterday; you can create other collections for convenient access to your files.

Files. When you choose a container in the Categories column, the Files column lists PDF files in that container.

Pages. When you choose a PDF file in the Files column, the Pages column shows you thumbnails of the pages in the document.

✔ Tip

■ You can zoom the thumbnails displayed in the Pages column. To do so, drag the slider beneath the thumbnail pane or click the + or – button (**Figure 12.2**).

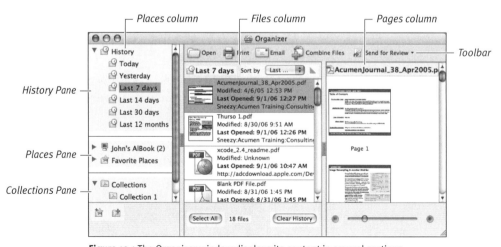

Figure 12.1 The Organizer window displays its content in several sections.

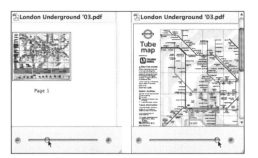

Figure 12.2 The slider beneath the Pages column zooms the page preview.

Open   Print   Email   Combine Files   Send for Review ▾

Figure 12.3 The Organizer window's toolbar gives you quick access to commonly used features.

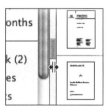

Figure 12.4 You can resize any of the columns by dragging the divider separating one column from the next.

Running along the top of the Files and Pages columns is a set of tool buttons that perform various actions on files you select in the Files column (**Figure 12.3**). These tools are duplicates of tools that exist in the Acrobat toolbars; we've discussed them elsewhere in this book. For the record, the tool buttons are as follows:

◆ Open opens the file selected in the Files column.

◆ Print prints the file selected in the Files column.

◆ Email uses your email client to send the selected file as an email attachment.

◆ Combine Files combines two or more selected files into a single PDF file or package. We described this in Chapter 4.

◆ Send for Review starts the review process for the select file. We discuss reviewing PDF files in Chapters 5–7.

✔ Tips

■ You can easily change the width of the columns in the Organizer window by dragging the dividers between the columns (**Figure 12.4**).

■ You can open a file by either selecting it in the Files column and then clicking the Open button, or double-clicking it in the Files column. I recommend double-clicking; it's faster.

EXAMINING THE ORGANIZER

Using the History Pane

The purpose of the History pane in the Places column (**Figure 12.5**) is to allow easy access to files you've looked at before.

The History pane gives you a useful variety of time periods from which to choose: Today, Yesterday, "Last 7 days," and so on.

Acrobat keeps track of all the documents you view and adds them to the appropriate time category. This happens without any intervention on your part.

To examine the files from a time period:

◆ Click the desired time period.

   The Files column lists all the files you viewed in that time period. For each file, Acrobat lists the name of the file, the date it was last modified and viewed, and the location of the file on the hard disk.

✔ Tip

■ You can sort the files in the Files column a variety of ways, including by filename, file size, and author. Choose the criterion from the "Sort by" pop-up menu.

Sometimes you may want to clear out Acrobat's internal list of files you've viewed. This may be for security purposes or just to simplify the list—the "Last 12 months" list can be so long that it isn't practical to find a particular file.

When you clear out Acrobat's history records, all the history categories become empty. Be certain you really want to do this, because it isn't undoable.

To clear the history:

◆ Click the Clear History button at the bottom of the Files column.

   Having cleared the history, Acrobat again starts accumulating files into the history categories.

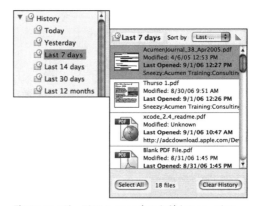

Figure 12.5 The History pane (top left) lets you view files according to when they were last viewed.

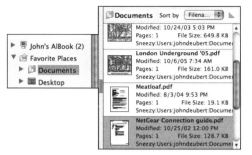

Figure 12.6 The Places pane (left) lets you view files according to where they're located on your computer.

Figure 12.7 You can add a new folder to the Places pane by clicking the New Favorites icon, located below the Places column.

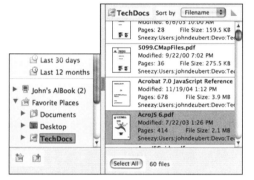

Figure 12.8 Once you've added a folder to the Places pane, you can see PDF files in that folder by clicking the folder's icon.

Figure 12.9 To delete a folder from the Favorite Places folder, right-click the folder and choose Remove from the contextual menu.

Using the Places Pane

The Places pane (**Figure 12.6**) lets you view places on your hard disk and server volumes that hold PDF files. Initially, this pane contains two folders:

◆ Your computer's disk, which may be opened to examine folders anywhere on your disk.

Opening this item gives you access to your entire hard disk's folder hierarchy.

◆ Favorite Places, where you can put folders that you frequently visit for PDF documents. This initially contains your Documents folder and your computer's Desktop.

The Favorite Places category is extremely useful if you have folders that contain libraries of PDF files. Add one of those folders to your favorites, and you can get to any of the files in that folder without having to work your way through your disk's file hierarchy.

To add a folder to the Favorite Places folder:

1. Click the New Favorites icon, beneath the Categories column, in the lower-left corner of the Organizer dialog box (**Figure 12.7**).

Your system's standard pick-a-folder dialog box opens.

2. Choose the folder on your disk that you want to add to your favorites.

Acrobat adds that folder to your favorites. From now on, you can access the contents of that folder by clicking the folder in the Favorite Places category (**Figure 12.8**).

To remove a folder from the Favorite Places folder:

1. Right-click the folder in the Favorite Places list to get to the contextual menu (**Figure 12.9**).

2. Choose the Remove item in the menu.

Acrobat removes the folder from your favorites.

Using the Collections Category

This is my favorite part of the Organizer. The Collections pane (**Figure 12.10**) lets you create collections of PDF documents that reside anywhere on your hard disk. If you have PDF files scattered here and there that pertain to a particular subject, you can place them all in a collection and access them from this virtual folder.

Initially, the Collections category has three "starter" collections, all of them empty, named Collection 1, Collection 2, and Collection 3. You can add files to these collections or create your own collection.

✔ Tip

■ You can rename collections, including the three default ones Adobe provides. To do so, click the collection name once to select it and then click it again to put the name into editing mode. Then, type the new name.

To create a new collection:

1. Click the New Collection icon, located beneath the Categories column (**Figure 12.11**).

   Acrobat inserts a new collection named something like Untitled 1.

2. Type a name for your collection.

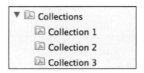

Figure 12.10 The Collections pane lists virtual folders that contain PDF files pertaining to a particular task.

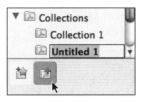

Figure 12.11 You create a new collection by clicking the New Collection icon below the Places column.

USING THE COLLECTIONS CATEGORY

Figure 12.12 You add files to a collection by right-clicking the collection and selecting Add Files from the contextual menu.

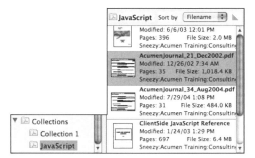

Figure 12.13 When you click a collection, the files it contains are displayed in the Files column.

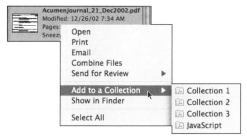

Figure 12.14 An alternative way of adding a file to a collection is to right-click the file in the Files pane, choose Add to a Collection, and choose the collection to which you want to add the file.

To add files to a collection:

1. Right-click the collection in the Categories column to obtain a contextual menu (**Figure 12.12**).

2. In the contextual menu, choose Add Files. Acrobat will present you with the standard pick-a-file dialog box.

3. Select the file you want to add to the collection.

   When you click the collection's name in the Category column, the Files column lists all the files you've placed in that collection (**Figure 12.13**).

✔ Tips

■ Note from Figure 12.12 that you can also rename or delete a collection by right-clicking it in the Categories column and choosing the appropriate option from the contextual menu.

■ An alternative way to add a file to a collection is to right-click that file in the Files column and choose Add to a Collection (**Figure 12.14**). The resulting contextual menu has a submenu that lists all existing collections; choose the collection to which you want to add the file.

CREATING
FORMS WITH
ACROBAT PRO

Acrobat Pro has long provided tools that let you define interactive form fields that can collect data from a reader and send that data back to you.

We could write an entire book (or two) about creating Acrobat forms. This chapter will introduce you to the basics of creating a functioning form with Acrobat. Happily, you can get very far with just the basics. Acrobat has added a large number of automated processes that create useful forms without your necessarily having to become an expert.

Much of this ease of use is a result of integration between Acrobat and Adobe LiveCycle Designer, a visual form editor that lets you create a form with the ease of laying out a page in a desktop publishing application. LiveCycle Designer is a separate program that ships with the Windows version (only) of Acrobat 8 Pro; it may also be purchased as a stand-alone forms generator.

Note that LiveCycle Designer isn't available in the Macintosh version of Acrobat. Bummer, but true. The biggest impact of this is that the Macintosh lacks access to Acrobat's form templates (more about these later). Still, the Mac version of Acrobat lets you create forms from electronic files and images, and it provides full support of the important form-distribution features. We'll talk about those as we go.

About LiveCycle Designer

Acrobat, together with LiveCycle Designer, lets you create forms from four sources:

- **Templates.** Acrobat provides a large collection of form templates that can be customized to your needs. This functionality is Windows only, because it requires LiveCycle Designer.

- **Electronic documents.** You can convert regular PDF files and scanned images of paper forms into interactive forms.

- **Excel spreadsheets.** Acrobat can convert Excel spreadsheets into forms. Again, this is Windows only.

- **Scanner.** Acrobat uses your scanner to convert a paper form into an image and from there to a PDF form.

We won't be discussing in detail the conversion of spreadsheets or scanning to a form. Once you understand the templates and, especially, converting electronic documents, the procedures for spreadsheets and scanners are relatively easy.

✔ Tip

- Forms created with LiveCycle Designer can't be dependably filled out with Acrobat 6 or earlier; the recipients of your form must have Acrobat 7 or later. If you need to make a form that is compatible with earlier versions of Acrobat, you must create your form fields by hand using the traditional Forms toolbar. This chapter ends with a brief introduction to this toolbar.

Figure 13.1 When you choose Forms > Create New Form, you are presented with a dialog box that lets you specify your starting point in the process.

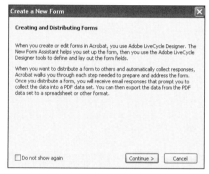

Figure 13.2 Acrobat reminds you that you are using LiveCycle Designer. Once you've read this a few dozen times, use the "Do not show again" check box.

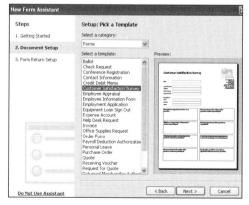

Figure 13.3 The second step in the wizard is to pick a template.

Using Form Templates

Most of the actions you'll take regarding forms—creating, distributing, collecting—are accessible through the aptly named Forms menu.

Let's start by creating a form from one of the large number of templates Acrobat supplies. This will give us an opportunity to examine LiveCycle Designer.

Again, the templates aren't available on the Macintosh.

To create a form from a template:

1. Choose Forms > Create New Form.

   Acrobat will display the first panel of the Create a New Form wizard (**Figure 13.1**).

2. Choose "Select a template," and click Continue.

   Acrobat displays an informational panel telling you about LiveCycle Designer (**Figure 13.2**). You should read this the first couple times, but then make use of the "Do not show again" check box.

3. Click Continue.

   The next panel of the Create New Form Wizard opens (**Figure 13.3**), and asks you to pick a template.

   Acrobat ships with an awe-inspiring collection of templates for everything from invoices to requests for unpaid leave.

   There is also a None selection, which drops you directly into LiveCycle Designer with a blank form.

4. Choose a category and a template within that category.

   The preview in the dialog box displays the template you choose.

   continues on next page

USING FORM TEMPLATES

5. Click Next.

The next step in the Create New Form wizard opens (**Figure 13.4**), which asks for your company name.

6. Type your company's name into the text, field and click Next.

The next panel asks for an image file containing your company's logo (**Figure 13.5**).

7. Click the Browse button, and choose the TIFF, JPEG, or other image file that contains your logo.

8. Click Next.

The next two panels ask for your company's contact information: address, telephone number, email address, and Web address.

9. Supply your company's address, and click Next.

10. Supply your telephone number and email and Web addresses, and click Next.

The final panel in the series asks whether your form should include an email button, a print button, or both (**Figure 13.6**).

11. Choose the "Add an email button" check box, and type your email address into the text box.

The email button allows recipients of the form to email their filled-out form to you. They click the Submit by Email button, and Acrobat uses their mail client to send you their responses.

You do want an email button; Acrobat's automated distribution and collection of forms depends on it.

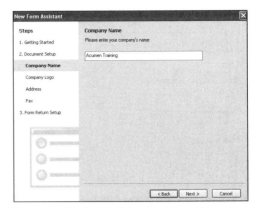

Figure 13.4 Acrobat needs to collect some information about your company for incorporation into the template. This includes your company's name and contact information.

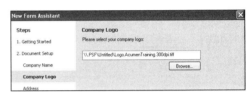

Figure 13.5 You can supply an image file that contains your company logo.

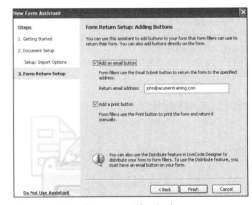

Figure 13.6 Finally, you specify whether you want an email button, a print button, or both.

12. If you want a print button, choose the "Add a print button" check box.

This button, of course, prints the form. The recipient can then send you the printed form by post or by fax.

13. Click Finish.

Acrobat thinks for a short while and then shows you your new form in LiveCycle designer (**Figure 13.7**).

14. Reposition and resize the form fields by dragging the fields and their handles (**Figure 13.8**).

You can also edit the field labels as you would any other text.

15. Choose File > Save to save the form.

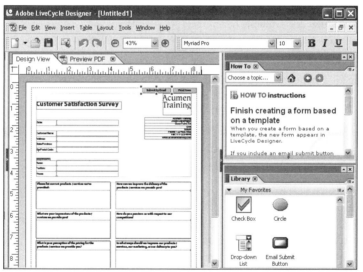

Figure 13.7 The LiveCycle Designer has three panes. Clockwise from left, these are the Design pane, the How To pane, and the Library pane.

Figure 13.8 When you create a form field, you can move it and resize it by dragging its border and its handles. You can also edit the label.

Editing Forms with LiveCycle Designer

When you have a form open in LiveCycle Designer, as at the end of the previous task, you're looking at a graphic representation of your form (Figure 13.7). The window has three panes:

How To (**Figure 13.9**). This pane presents a complete and useable help system for LiveCycle Designer. Refer to this early and often.

Library (**Figure 13.10**). This pane supplies form fields and controls you can place on your Acrobat page. Choose a control type, and then click the form page to place a form field. (We'll discuss this more later.)

Design. This pane presents a view of your form's page. Two views are available here; select one by clicking the appropriate tab at the top of the pane:

♦ The Design View pane presents the page in editable format. This is the view you use to place your form fields (**Figure 13.11**).

♦ The Preview PDF pane shows what the final form will look like when filled out in Acrobat (**Figure 13.12**).

Most of the time, you'll use LiveCycle Designer to adjust the position and size of form fields created by one of the templates, as you did in the previous section. You can also place your own form fields on the page.

✔ Tip

■ The Library pane supplies controls (such as push buttons) as well as data fields (like check boxes and lists). In Acrobat parlance, these are all referred to as *form fields*.

Figure 13.9 The How To pane supplies access to a complete, easy-to-use help system.

Figure 13.10 The Library pane provides tools to place various type of form fields on the page.

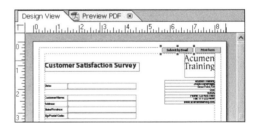

Figure 13.11 The Design pane shows you your form in an editable state. You can move, resize, and otherwise edit the form fields.

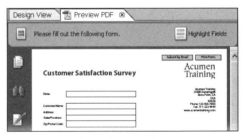

Figure 13.12 The Preview PDF pane shows you how the form will look to the person who fills it out.

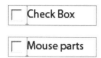

Figure 13.13 When you first place a form field, it has a generic label (top). Edit this label text so it's the way you want it on the form.

Figure 13.14 You can reposition and resize the form field by dragging the border or its handles.

Figure 13.15 If you make the label's box too short, the label may wrap to multiple lines.

To place a form field on the page:

1. In the Library pane, click the form field type that you want to add to the page.

2. Click the page in the Design View pane to indicate where you want the control to go.

   Acrobat places the new control on the page with a generic label (**Figure 13.13**).

3. Select the label's text as you would in a text editor, and change the label to whatever you want (Figure 13.13).

4. Click the border of the control to get a border rectangle and handles (**Figure 13.14**).

5. Reposition and resize the form field by dragging the border and its handles.

✔ Tip

- If you reduce the width of your control too much, LiveCycle Designer wraps the label to a second line (**Figure 13.15**).

Having placed your form field, you can modify quite a few of its visual characteristics by right-clicking the field. For example, you can specify the font of the form field and its label.

To change a field's text properties:

1. Right-click the form field to display its contextual menu.

2. Choose Palettes > Font (**Figure 13.16**). The Font palette opens (**Figure 13.17**).

3. From the pop-up menus, choose the font and size you want for the label's text.

    You can also choose from a variety of styles, such as bold and italic.

4. Click the Windows close box to dismiss the palette when you're finished.

✔ Tips

■ If you click the Paragraph tab in the Font palette, you can change a number of properties affecting the placement of the label text (**Figure 13.18**). Many of these paragraph properties have an effect only if the label text has wrapped to multiple lines.

■ There are a number of other palettes available from the contextual menu (Figure 13.16). The most routinely useful one is the Border palette, which lets you change the appearance of the form field's border.

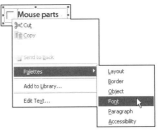

Figure 13.16 You can change a variety of a control's properties with contextual-menu options. Here we're changing the font.

Figure 13.17 The Font palette lets you change the font, size, and style of the form field's label.

Figure 13.18 If you click the Paragraph tab, you can specify the label's alignment, as well as other, less-frequently used properties.

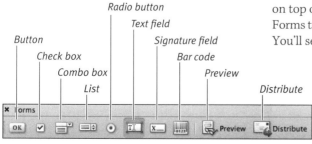

Figure 13.19 When you convert an electronic document to a form, your starting document looks like a form but isn't one. The lines and squares are just lines and squares, not form fields.

Converting Electronic Documents to Forms

Many corporations today find themselves with a collection of paper forms that they want to convert to PDF forms that can be filled out electronically.

Acrobat 8 has made this a much easier task than it was in earlier versions. The only prerequisite is that the form must be in electronic format. It must be scanned or, if it was designed with software, it must be exported to PDF. The resulting PDF or image file looks like a form (**Figure 13.19**), but there are no active form fields on the page; the lines are just graphic lines.

Converting the electronic file to a PDF interactive form is easy. Acrobat 8's new Form Field Recognition feature opens the file, analyzes it, and automatically places appropriate form fields on the new PDF page. You'll probably need to add some additional form fields manually using LiveCycle Designer or the Acrobat Forms toolbar; the analysis often fails to recognize some of the fill-in spaces in the original document.

Still, Acrobat does an amazingly good job for a first pass; you're left, relatively speaking, with just clean-up.

I'm pleased to report that this feature is available on the Macintosh as well as in Windows. Mac users need to do their touch-up with the Acrobat Forms tools (**Figure 13.20**) rather than with LiveCycle Designer. That's all right, because it's arguably easier to lay form fields on top of existing artwork using the Acrobat Forms tools than it is with LiveCycle Designer. You'll see how to do this later in the chapter.

Figure 13.20 Because Acrobat doesn't supply LiveCycle Designer for the Macintosh, Mac users touch up converted documents with the Forms toolbar.

To convert an electronic file into a form:

1. Choose Forms > Create New Form.

   The Create a New Form dialog box opens (**Figure 13.21**).

2. Choose the "Start with an electronic document" radio button, and click Continue.

   Acrobat presents you with the first pane in the Create a New Form wizard, which asks you to locate the document you want to convert (**Figure 13.22**).

3. Click the Browse button, and choose the PDF or image file you want to convert; then, click the Next button.

   Acrobat displays a progress bar and spends some time importing the document. Although this process is usually fast, it can sometimes take a remarkably long time, so don't cancel the process until several minutes have elapsed.

4. When Acrobat is finished processing the file, click the Next button.

   Acrobat takes you to step 3 of the wizard (**Figure 13.23**), which asks if Acrobat should automatically place form fields on the page or if you want to place them all by hand.

   You want to use auto-detection. It always gives you a head start and rarely can hurt you. Plus, it's cool.

5. Choose the Run Auto Field Detection radio button, and click Next.

   Acrobat spends some time (usually not much) analyzing the file and placing form fields where it thinks they should go. Eventually, it tells you it's done (**Figure 13.24**).

6. Click the Next button.

   A final message appears, with a Done button at the bottom.

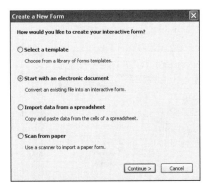

Figure 13.21 To convert a PDF file or scanned paper form to an Acrobat form, choose "Start with an electronic document."

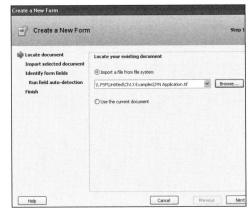

Figure 13.22 The first step of the wizard asks you to pick the document you want to convert.

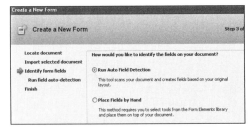

Figure 13.23 Acrobat then asks if you want it to automatically place form fields on the page. You do.

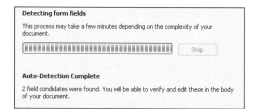

Figure 13.24 Acrobat presents a progress bar while it analyzes your document and places form fields on the page.

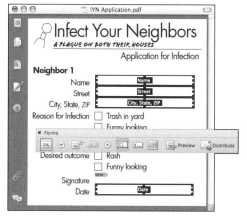

Figure 13.25 Having added form fields to the page, Acrobat opens the page in LiveCycle designer or, on the Mac, makes the Forms toolbar visible.

7. Click the Done button.

   In Windows, Acrobat opens your new form in LiveCycle Designer. On the Mac, Acrobat opens the new form in a document window and makes the Forms toolbar visible (**Figure 13.25**).

   You see form fields placed on the page in all the places Acrobat decided form fields should go. It may miss some, but it does a good job overall.

8. Add the missing form fields using either LiveCycle Designer (Windows) or the Forms toolbar (Mac).

   I consider this easier to do with the Forms toolbar; since the artwork is already on the page, the Forms tools are more streamlined for this stage of the task. We'll look at creating a form field with the Forms tools later in the chapter.

9. Reposition and resize the existing form fields.

10. When all is to your liking, save the PDF form by selecting File > Save.

✔ Tips

■ If you have a document already open in Acrobat when you start the wizard, you can choose the "Use the current document" button, located just below the pathname field in Figure 13.22.

■ LiveCycle Designer uses a different internal format for its form fields than the long-standing PDF format. As a result, you can't edit forms created with LiveCycle Designer with the Acrobat Forms toolbar. However, LiveCycle designer can edit form fields created with the Forms toolbar.

Adding a Form Field with the Forms Toolbar

Before LiveCycle Designer, there was the Forms toolbar. This is how form fields have been added to PDF pages since Acrobat 4.

The tools in this toolbar let you create form fields, move them around the page, and otherwise do the tasks essential to creating a form. The Forms tools presume that the labels and other artwork already exist on the PDF page. You use the tools to lay form fields on top of the artwork.

We'll look at the basic steps involved in creating a form field. These are all you need for the most common fields: check boxes and text fields.

To add a form field using the Forms toolbar:

1. With your PDF file open, in the Forms toolbar, click the type of form field you want to add (Figure 13.20).

   The mouse pointer turns into a crosshairs.

2. Drag out a rectangle corresponding to the new form field's position (**Figure 13.26**).

   The Field Properties dialog box opens (**Figure 13.27**). This dialog box has tabs that differ for the different form field types, although the General, Appearance, and Actions tabs are always present.

   For a basic form field, as we're constructing here, you can ignore most of the controls; the default values are fine. We'll look at the controls you'll most frequently want to change for a simple check box or text field.

Figure 13.26 As you drag out your form field, it appears as a red rectangle with handles.

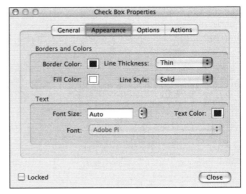

Figure 13.27 The Field Properties dialog box (here for a check box) lets you specify the appearance and other properties of a form field.

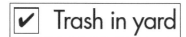

Figure 13.28 When you return to the Acrobat Hand tool, your form field is in place and functioning on the page.

3. Click the Appearance tab (Figure 13.27).

4. Choose a Border Color and a Fill Color, if you want one of them.

   You'll probably want to set these to None; remember that you're laying these fields over existing artwork.

5. Choose a font and size for the text in your field.

   For text fields, you may choose any font on your system and any size you wish. A size of "Auto" uses the largest font size that lets the text fit vertically in the text field.

   You can't choose a font or a size for a check box; these are dictated by the needs of the field.

6. Click OK to finish your form field definition.

   Your form field is still visible on the document page as a red rectangle with handles (Figure 13.26).

7. Reposition and resize the form field to make it match the page's artwork.

8. Click the Acrobat Hand tool (or any other tool) to finish your field definition.

   The form field is now in place on the page (**Figure 13.28**).

✔ **Tip**

■ In step 7, you can use the arrow keys to nudge the position of the form field by 1 pixel. If you hold down the Shift key, the arrows nudge the field's size.

Adding a Submit Button Using the Forms Toolbar

One important field that Macintosh users need to add to their forms is a Submit button that submits the form to an email address. Acrobat needs one of these to be able to automatically distribute and collect forms. Creating the button isn't hard, but it does entail a fair number of steps.

Buttons frequently don't have corresponding artwork already on the page. The following steps assume that the page is blank where the button should go.

The following task also assumes your form file is open in Acrobat and the Forms toolbar is visible.

To create a Submit button:

1. Click the Button tool in the Forms toolbar.

   The mouse pointer turns into a crosshairs.

2. Drag out a rectangle corresponding to where you want the button to go.

   The Button Properties dialog box opens (**Figure 13.29**). You can accept the default values for most of this dialog box's controls, but to make a Submit button, you need to make some specific selections. Any controls I don't mention may be left with their default values.

3. In the Appearance tab, set the Border Color to black and the Fill Color to whatever looks nice to you.

4. Set the Line Style pop-up menu to Beveled and set the Font and Font Size to whatever you wish.

5. Click the Options tab.

   Acrobat displays controls specific to a button's appearance (**Figure 13.30**).

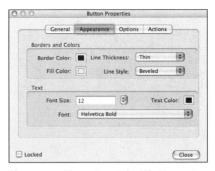

Figure 13.29 To create a Submit button, set the Border Color to black, the Fill Color to whatever is pretty, and the Line Style to Beveled.

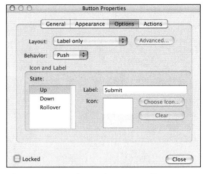

Figure 13.30 In the Options pane for your Submit button, set the Behavior to Push, and type Submit into the Label text box.

Figure 13.31 In the Submit button's Actions pane, choose "Submit a form" for the Action, and then click the Add button.

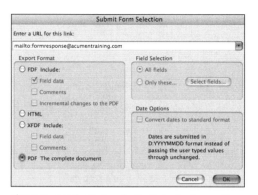

Figure 13.32 In the Options for the Submit a Form action, type your email address into the URL text box and choose the "PDF The complete document" radio button.

Figure 13.33 When you return to the Button Properties dialog box, "Submit a form" appears as the button's action.

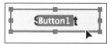

Figure 13.34 Returning to the document page, reposition and resize the button.

Figure 13.35 When you return to the Acrobat Hand tool, your Submit button, fully functional, resides on the page.

6. In the Behavior pop-up menu, choose Push and in the Label text box, type the label you want for the button. Submit is a reasonable choice.

7. Click the Actions tab.

These controls specify what the button should do (**Figure 13.31**).

8. In the Select Trigger pop-up menu, choose Mouse Up and in the Select Action pop-up menu, choose "Submit a form," then click the Add button.

The Submit Form Selection dialog box opens (**Figure 13.32**).

9. In the "Enter a URL for this link" text box, type the form's return email address preceded by mailto:.

Thus, if the return email address is a@b.com, you type mailto:a@b.com.

10. For Export Format, choose the "PDF The complete document" radio button then click OK.

Acrobat returns you to the Button Properties dialog box, now showing your "Submit a form" action in the Actions area (**Figure 13.33**).

11. Click Close.

Acrobat returns you to your document, now showing your button as a red rectangle with handles (**Figure 13.34**).

12. Reposition and resize the button as you wish by dragging the rectangle and its handles.

13. Click the Acrobat Hand tool (or any other tool) to see your functioning Submit button (**Figure 13.35**).

Whew! When the user clicks this button, Acrobat emails the form and its data to the address you specified.

ADDING A SUBMIT BUTTON USING FORMS TOOLBAR

Distributing Forms

In times past, one of the most troublesome parts of using Acrobat for your forms was distributing them and then somehow getting information back from your respondents.

Acrobat 8 has made it admirably simple to distribute a form and collect its responses by email. The one requirement is that your form must have a Submit button created in LiveCycle Designer or the Forms toolbar. (See Acrobat Help for more instructions on creating buttons.)

When you distribute a form, Acrobat creates a *dataset file* that it uses to keep track of responses returned for the form. Acrobat does all the bookkeeping associated with collecting and collating the form data. At any time, you can open the dataset file in Acrobat and see all the responses that have been returned so far.

As one who has worked with people for years setting up form distribution and response workflows, let me assure you this is way cool.

The following task assumes you have your form document open in Acrobat.

To distribute a form by email:

1. Choose Forms > Distribute Form.

   The Form Distribution Options dialog box opens (**Figure 13.36**). This dialog box allows you to choose between having Acrobat email the form to its recipients immediately or saving the file so you can email it yourself later.

2. Choose "Send now via email," and then click OK.

   Acrobat displays step 1 of the Distribute Form Wizard (**Figure 13.37**). It asks for the email address to which responses should be returned.

Figure 13.36 When you choose Forms > Distribute a Form, Acrobat presents you with a dialog box that lets you distribute your form by email.

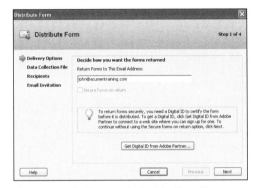

Figure 13.37 The first step in the Distribute Form Wizard asks for your return email address. This is where responses will be sent.

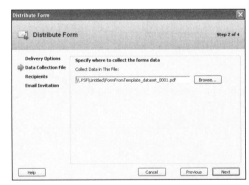

Figure 13.38 In step 2, the Distribute Form Wizard asks you to name the data collection file that Acrobat will use to keep track of incoming responses.

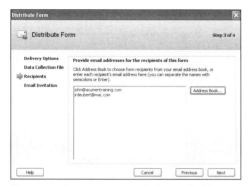

Figure 13.39 In step 3, you supply the email addresses of the people to whom the form should be sent.

Figure 13.40 Finally, you provide text for the outgoing email's subject and message body. When you click the Done button, your form is sent.

Figure 13.41 A person who receives your form sees a brief set of instructions at the top of the form's page.

3. Type the email address for responses into the pane, and click Next.

Step 2 of the wizard appears (**Figure 13.38**), which asks for the name and location of the dataset file.

4. Click the Browse button, and specify a location and name for the dataset file in the Save dialog box.

5. Click Next.

The next step in the wizard (**Figure 13.39**) asks you for the email addresses of the form's recipients. This step will be missing if you earlier opted to email the form yourself rather than let Acrobat do it.

6. Type into the text field the email addresses of all the people to whom the form should be sent.

The addresses may be on separate lines within the field or separated by semicolons. Note that you can also click the Address Book button and take addresses from your system's address book.

7. Click Next.

Acrobat takes you to the final step in the wizard, which asks for a subject and message body for your email message (**Figure 13.40**).

8. Type a subject and message into the appropriate fields, and click Done.

Acrobat mails your form as an attachment to the email addresses you provided.

When recipients receive the emailed form and open it in Acrobat, they see an instruction panel at the top of the document panel (**Figure 13.41**). This text is pretty basic, telling the recipient to fill out the form.

Having filled out the form, the recipient clicks the Submit by Email button; Acrobat uses the recipient's mail client to send the completed form back to you (or, rather, to the email address you supplied when you distributed the form).

Receiving Forms

Acrobat 8 also makes it remarkably easy to receive and compile responses to your form. The secret is the bookkeeping it maintains in the form's dataset, which is created when you distribute the form. As you receive emailed responses, Acrobat checks to see to which dataset they belong and adds the responses to all the others for that form.

The whole process has become a breeze instead of a chore.

To receive a completed form:

1. In your mail software, open the email with the attached, completed form.

2. Open the attached PDF file.

   In most systems, you can do this directly from the email client. In other systems, you may need to download the attachment to a file and then open that.

   A dialog box opens, notifying you that the form belongs to a dataset and asking permission to add the form to that dataset (**Figure 13.42**).

3. Click OK.

   Acrobat adds the form's responses to the dataset. You're now looking at the completed form, which you can examine, if you wish.

Figure 13.42 When you open a completed form, Acrobat asks you if it may add the form's data to the dataset it created when you distributed the form. Tell it OK.

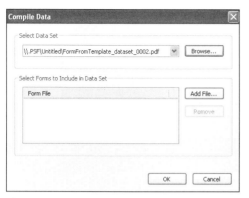

Figure 13.43 The Compile Data dialog box asks you to choose the dataset whose responses you want to browse.

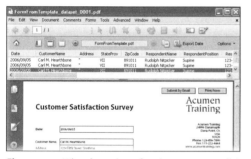

Figure 13.44 When browsing a form's responses, a list of recipients appears at the top of the form window. Clicking a name in the list displays that person's data.

To view the responses from all the forms returned so far, you open the dataset in Acrobat. The software will display a document window that has a pane listing of all of the recipients. Click on an entry in the list to see that responder's form entries.

To view the responses for all returned forms:

1. Choose Forms > Compile Returned Forms. The Compile Data dialog box opens (**Figure 13.43**).

2. Click the Browse button, and choose the dataset whose responses you want to view.

3. If you want to add additional, individual PDF form files to the dataset (that you haven't opened and added already), click the Add File button, and choose the individual PDF files from the resulting Open dialog box.

4. Click OK.

    Acrobat displays a PDF document window that has a pane listing the recipients whose data are in the dataset (**Figure 13.44**).

5. Click a recipient's name in the list to see that person's responses.

6. Close the window when you're done.

✔ Tips

- You can click any of the headings in the list of customers in Figure 13.44 to sort the list by that field, such as CustomerName or RespondentPosition.

- If you click the Export Data button, which is above the list in Figure 13.44, a standard Save dialog box opens that lets you save the image data as comma-delimited text. This file is suitable for importing into a spreadsheet or a database manager so you can further analyze the data.

RECEIVING FORMS

PASSWORD PROTECTION

An increasing proportion of the world's documents are distributed as PDF files, many of which are to a greater or lesser extent confidential. Banks don't want their customers' financial statements read by just anyone; software companies need to keep new product specifications from the eyes of their competitors; and most of us don't want our love letters broadcast for the world to read.

Acrobat offers three types of security to control the opening and viewing of a PDF file:

Password security. You assign a password that is required to open the file. This is simple and effective and is the method we'll discuss in this chapter.

Certificate security. This approach restricts the reading of the file to a specific list of people. Each person on the list must have a *digital ID*, which we'll discuss in Chapter 15.

LiveCycle Policy Server security. Adobe LiveCycle Policy Server is software that manages digital IDs and permissions on a server. This allows permissions to be restricted or loosened on the fly by an administrator.

You can also restrict the actions a viewer can perform with the document and require a password to overcome those restrictions. Thus, readers may be able to open a file but not print it unless they know the Secret Word.

Restricting File Access

The most effective protection you can apply to a file is to password-protect access to it; viewers may not see the file's contents unless they know the password. The file is encrypted, so that even if you open it with a text editor and try to look at the PDF code (always a treat), all you see is gibberish.

The encryption applied to the file's contents has gotten more sophisticated as Acrobat has matured. The more secure your document is, the later the version of Acrobat a reader must have to open it.

To password-restrict access to a document:

1. With the document open, choose File > Properties.

The Document Properties dialog box opens (**Figure 14.1**). Choose the Security tab.

2. In the Security Method pop-up menu, choose Password Security.

The Password Security-Settings dialog box opens (**Figure 14.2**).

3. In the Compatibility pop-up menu, choose the earliest version of Acrobat a reader

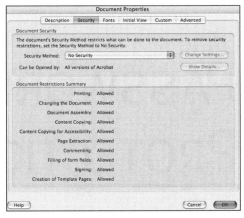

Figure 14.1 The Document Properties dialog box's Security pane allows you to specify what method to use to secure your document.

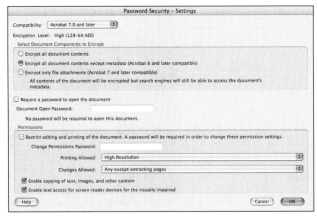

Figure 14.2: The Password Security-Settings dialog box has all the controls to restrict access to your document.

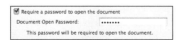

Figure 14.3 To prevent your document from being opened by unauthorized personnel, type a password into the Document Open Password text box.

Figure 14.4 When you close the Password Security-Settings dialog box, Acrobat will ask you to confirm your password.

can have and still be able to open the document.

Here you decide how strong the encryption applied to your document must be; later versions of Acrobat use stronger encryption than earlier versions.

You may choose compatibility with Acrobat 3, 5, 6, or 7. The later the version of Acrobat you require, the harder it will be to read your encrypted content, but also the more often you'll have readers who can't read your document without updating their Acrobat or Reader software.

4. Decide what parts within your document should be encrypted: everything, everything except metadata, or nothing except attached files.

    See the sidebar "What to Encrypt?" for a discussion of what to encrypt. Personally, I tend to encrypt everything.

5. Check the "Require a password to open the document" check box.

6. Type a password into the Document Open Password text box (**Figure 14.3**).

    Note that the password you type appears as a row of bullets on the screen.

7. Click OK.

    A dialog box opens, asking you to confirm your password (**Figure 14.4**).

8. Type your password into the text box, and click OK.

    Acrobat returns you to the Document Properties dialog box, which now displays your security settings.

9. Click OK to return to your PDF document.

continues on next page

RESTRICTING FILE ACCESS

✔ Tips

■ The document isn't actually password protected until you save it to your disk. Until you do so, you can freely change your security settings by clicking the Change Settings button in the Document Properties dialog box (Figure 14.1).

■ When readers attempt to open your protected file, they're asked for a password (**Figure 14.5**). If they type an incorrect password, they aren't allowed to open the file.

Figure 14.5 When someone opens your password-protected document, Acrobat demands the password of them.

What to Encrypt?

When you assign an Open password to a document, Acrobat encrypts the contents of the document, making it impossible to read the document without knowing the password. Acrobat gives you three choices in deciding how much of your PDF file to encrypt (**Figure 14.6**):

◆ **Encrypt all document contents.** Acrobat encrypts everything in your file. This is the option I generally choose because it has the lowest requirements for reading the document: A reader must have only Acrobat 5 or later.

◆ **Encrypt all document contents except metadata.** Acrobat leaves keywords and other metadata unencrypted so that they're searchable. This requires the reader to have Acrobat 6 or later.

◆ **Encrypt only file attachments.** The Comments toolbar allows you to attach a spreadsheet or other file to your document. These attached files are encrypted, but nothing else is. This requires at least Acrobat 7 to be read.

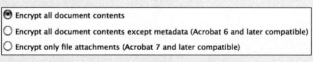

Figure 14.6 You have control over what parts of your password-protected document are encrypted.

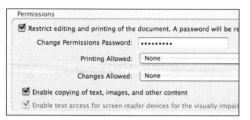

Figure 14.7 The Permissions controls let you specify the degree to which readers may edit your document.

Restricting Reader Activities

Acrobat allows you to restrict what readers can do with your file once they have opened it. The Permissions controls in the Password Security Settings dialog box (**Figure 14.7**) allow you to restrict the editing and printing of your file and to assign a password that must be typed in before the permissions can be changed.

These permissions and their password are completely independent of the password needed to open the document. You can have an Open password, a Permissions password, both, or neither.

You can allow three levels of printing permission:

◆ **High Resolution.** This option allows unrestricted printing of the document.

◆ **Low Resolution.** The document is always printed as a 150 dpi bitmap. Thus, a reader can print a proof of this document but not a high-quality copy.

◆ **None.** The document may not be printed.

Editing permissions

You can also allow one of five degrees of permission for editing the file:

- **None.** The reader isn't allowed to modify the file.

- **Inserting, deleting, and rotating pages.** This option is self explanatory.

- **Filling in form fields and signing existing signature fields.** This option is appropriate for a distributed form. It allows recipients to input information into a questionnaire but prevents them from playfully changing the wording of the questions using the TouchUp tools.

- **Commenting, filling in form fields, and signing existing signature fields.** This option lets readers fill in a form and attach comments. Thus, an expense report form allows the attachment of scanned receipts (as an "attachment" comment).

- **Any except extracting pages.** Readers can do any modification of the document they wish except pulling the pages out into another document. Note that readers can use the TouchUp tools to change the content of the PDF file.

In addition to these editing and printing permissions, you may allow readers to copy text and other content from your file and, presumably, paste it into another document.

Finally, if you restrict copying of the content of your document, you may nonetheless allow screen readers and other devices for the visually impaired to extract the text.

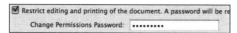

Figure 14.8 You must supply a password to restrict the editing of your file.

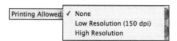

Figure 14.9 You may forbid a reader to print your document, allow a low-resolution proof, or allow full-quality printing.

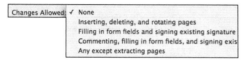

Figure 14.10 You may choose from among a variety of degrees to which a user may modify your PDF file.

One important fact about these permissions is that obeying the restrictions is the responsibility of the PDF viewing software, which includes not only the Adobe Acrobat products but also such programs as Apple's Preview and the free Ghostscript program. The permissions exist as a series of flags in the PDF file that tell the PDF viewer which actions are restricted and which are allowed. Absolutely nothing enforces these restrictions; if a PDF viewer chooses to ignore them, then it may allow its user to print, edit, and otherwise modify the PDF file regardless of the permissions settings.

To assign permissions to a document:

1. With the document open, choose File > Properties.

   Acrobat will display the Document Properties dialog box (Figure 14.1).

2. In the Security Method pop-up menu, choose Password Security.

   The Password Security - Settings dialog box opens (Figure 14.2).

2. Choose the "Restrict editing and printing" check box (**Figure 14.8**).

3. Type a password into the Change Permissions Password field.

   As usual, the password you type appears as a row of bullets on the screen.

4. Choose the degree of printing permission you want from the Printing Allowed pop-up menu (**Figure 14.9**).

5. From the Changes Allowed pop-up, choose the permission you wish to allow for editing your file (**Figure 14.10**).

continues on next page

RESTRICTING READER ACTIVITIES

6. If you want to allow readers to copy text and images from your PDF file, choose the "Enable copying..." check box.

7. If you choose to *not* allow readers to copy text from your file, but you still want screen readers for the visually impaired to work, then choose the "Enable text access..." check box.

This check box is disabled if you allow text copying.

8. Click OK.

Acrobat asks you to confirm your password (**Figure 14.11**).

9. Type your password into the text box, and click OK.

Acrobat returns you to the Document Properties dialog box.

10. Click OK to return to the document page.

The permissions aren't actually set until you save the PDF file. Until then, you may click the Change Settings button in the Document Properties dialog box and modify your permissions.

Once you've saved your file, the Document Properties dialog box reflects your security settings (**Figure 14.12**).

Figure 14.11 When you close the Password Security Settings dialog box, Acrobat asks you to confirm your password.

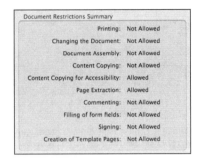

Figure 14.12 Once you've saved your document, the Permissions settings are put in place and the Document Properties dialog box reflects this.

15

DIGITAL SIGNATURES

From the early days, Adobe has wanted contracts and other agreements in PDF format to be legally binding documents. To do this, there needed to be some way of electronically signing a PDF document so that it was unimpeachably certain that a particular person had agreed to its contents.

At this point, the problem has been solved; electronically signed PDF files are accepted as legally binding documents by many federal agencies and state governments, including the Internal Revenue Service and the State of California. In this chapter, we shall see how to sign a PDF document and how to confirm that the signature on a signed document is valid.

About Adobe Self-Sign Security

Acrobat's electronic signature mechanism is open-ended. Third-party companies, such as Cyber-SIGN and Entrust, can implement their own ways of identifying the signer of a document using Adobe Acrobat's plug-in technology.

In this chapter, we'll discuss the use of the electronic signature mechanism that ships with Acrobat: Adobe Self-Sign Security. It has become easier to use in Acrobat 8 than in earlier versions.

You need to understand the following concepts and terms before you can use Adobe Self-Sign Security:

Digital ID. A collection of data that electronically identifies a person. This is the data that is embedded in the signed document to identify the signer.

Certificate. A file that contains digital ID information. This file can be sent to another person for installation into their copy of Acrobat as a *trusted identity*.

Trusted identity. A certificate that has been installed in your copy of Acrobat and can be used to validate a signature. It's "trusted" in the sense that you know the certificate actually came from the person whom it's supposed to represent.

Signature validation. The process of confirming that a signature was created with a particular digital ID. When you receive a signed document, validation confirms that the signature was created by a person who is among your trusted identities.

Setting up to use signatures

Some preparation must be accomplished before you can digitally sign PDF documents. We'll examine each of these steps in greater detail later in the chapter:

- You create on your computer a digital ID that you'll use to sign documents. You must also create a password that you'll need to enter every time you use this ID.

- You create a certificate from this digital ID.

- You send the certificate to people who might be recipients of your signed documents.

- The people to whom you send your certificate must import it into their copies of Acrobat as a trusted identity that represents you as a signer.

   They should also confirm that it was you who sent the certificate, perhaps by calling you on the telephone and asking if you just emailed a certificate to them.

With this preparation in place, signing a document is relatively easy:

- You supply your digital ID and password; the ID's identifying information is embedded in the signature.

- You send your signed document to a recipient.

- The recipient validates the signature, confirming that it corresponds to your certificate and, therefore, really was placed on the document by you.

Let's see how to accomplish all this.

ABOUT ADOBE SELF-SIGN SECURITY

Creating a Digital ID

The first bit of preparation you must do when you intend to sign one or more PDF documents is to create a digital ID. You can do this on the fly when you sign a document, but if signing a document will be a common activity for you, you should create your ID ahead of time.

To create a digital ID:

1. Choose Advanced > Security Settings.

   The Security Settings dialog box opens (**Figure 15.1**).

2. Click the Digital IDs heading in the column on the left side of the dialog box.

   Acrobat displays all the digital IDs currently defined on this computer. This list is initially blank, of course.

3. Click the Add ID icon.

   The first panel of the Add Digital ID Wizard opens (**Figure 15.2**), which asks how you want to create your ID.

4. Choose the "Create a self-signed digital ID for use with Acrobat" radio button, and click Next.

   The next panel (**Figure 15.3**) wants to know whether the ID you create should be stored as a file or in the Windows Certificate Store. For the purpose of this book, the digital file is preferable, because it's a cross-platform industry standard.

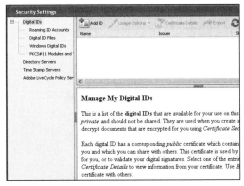

Figure 15.1 You create a digital ID by going to the Security Settings dialog box.

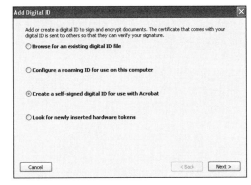

Figure 15.2 In the Add Digital ID dialog box, you tell Acrobat that you want to make a self-signed ID.

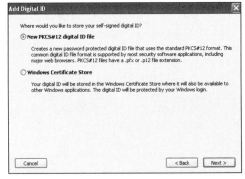

Figure 15.3 You can store your digital ID as a standard-format file or in the Windows Certificate Store. The latter works only in Windows, of course.

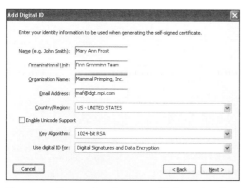

Figure 15.4 You can type in personal information that may be displayed as part of your digital signature. You should supply at least your name.

Figure 15.5 Type in a password that you'll need to supply whenever you sign a document.

5. Choose "New PKCS#12 digital ID file," and click Next.

   The next panel (**Figure 15.4**) asks for some professional information, such as your name and title. This information can be displayed as part of your signature.

6. Type in as much of the information as you like (I suggest at least your name), and click Next.

   Acrobat will display the next panel (**Figure 15.5**), which asks where the data file for the ID should be placed (there's no good reason not to accept the default); it also asks for a password.

7. Type a password into the Password and Confirm Password fields, and click Finish.

   You'll need to supply this password every time you sign a document.

   When you click the Finish button, Acrobat returns you to the Security Settings dialog box, which now displays your new digital ID (**Figure 15.6**).

8. Click the standard Close button to finish the process.

Figure 15.6 When you return to the Security Settings dialog box, it lists your new digital ID.

Creating a Certificate from an ID

A certificate is a digital file you can send to the people to whom you'll be sending signed documents. They can import this certificate into their copies of Acrobat to create a trusted identity, which represents you to their systems.

To create a certificate:

1. Choose Advanced > Security Settings.

   The Security Settings dialog box opens.

2. Click the Digital IDs heading in the column on the left side of the dialog box.

   Acrobat displays all the digital IDs currently defined on this computer.

3. Click the digital ID from which you want to create a certificate.

   Acrobat displays information about the person whose ID this is (**Figure 15.7**).

4. Click the Export icon at the top of the dialog box (**Figure 15.8**).

   Acrobat will display the Export Options dialog box (**Figure 15.9**). This dialog box presents you with the choice of exporting your certificate as a file or immediately emailing the certificate to someone.

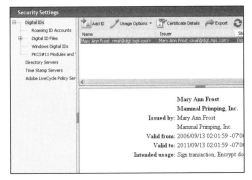

Figure 15.7 You create a certificate for your digital ID from the Security Settings dialog box.

Figure 15.8 Choose your digital ID in the Security Settings dialog box, and click the Export icon.

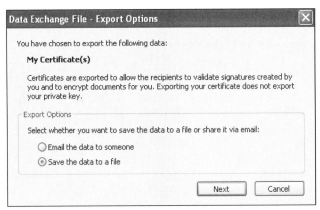

Figure 15.9 Acrobat gives you the choice of saving your certificate to a file or immediately emailing it to someone.

5. Choose the "Save the data to a file" radio button, and click Next.

A standard Save dialog box opens.

6. Specify a name and location on your disk for the certificate file, and click OK.

Acrobat creates the certificate file in the location you specify. You now have a file that you can send to recipients of your signed documents.

✔ Tip

■ If you choose the "Email the data to someone" radio button in step 5, Acrobat creates a certificate and immediately emails it to a recipient. When you click the Next button, the Compose Email dialog box opens (**Figure 15.10**), which lets you supply an address, a subject, and a message body for the email.

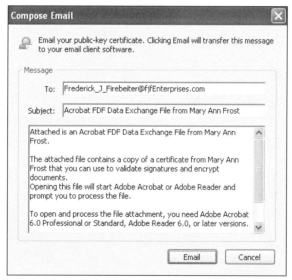

Figure 15.10 If you have Acrobat email your certificate, the software asks for an address and subject for the email. You can also modify the mail's message body.

CREATING A CERTIFICATE FROM AN ID

Importing a Certificate as a Trusted Identity

In the previous section, you created a certificate that encapsulates your digital ID. When you send this file to another person—presumably someone to whom you'll be sending electronically signed documents—they must import the certificate into Acrobat as a trusted identity.

The presence of a trusted identity allows Acrobat to identify the signer of a PDF document. Acrobat can confirm that a digital signature was placed on the page by the same person who is identified by the trusted identity.

The trusted identity is "trusted" in the sense that you know it really came from the person it claims to represent. This can be confirmed relatively simply: Telephone the person who you believe sent you the certificate, and ask that person if they sent you a certificate.

The following task assumes the certificate file is somewhere on your hard disk. If the file was emailed to you, you need to save the email attachment to your disk.

To import a certificate as a trusted identity:

1. Choose Advanced > Manage Trusted Identities.

   Acrobat will present you with the Manage Trusted Identities dialog box (**Figure 15.11**).

   This dialog box lists all the trusted identities your copy of Acrobat knows about.

2. Click the Add Contacts button.

   The Choose Contacts to Import dialog box opens (**Figure 15.12**). This dialog box allows you to choose as many certificates as you wish to import into your copy of Acrobat.

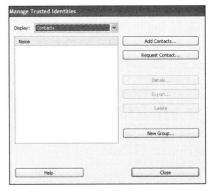

Figure 15.11 To import a certificate as a trusted identity, you go to the Manage Trusted Identities dialog box and click Add Contacts.

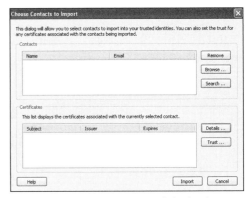

Figure 15.12 The Choose Contacts dialog box lets you choose a certificate to import. Just click the Browse button and choose the certificate file.

Figure 15.13 Once you've selected a certificate, the name of the contact appears in the Choose Contacts dialog box.

Figure 15.14 To specify the actions for which the identity should be trusted, choose the contact, and click the Details button.

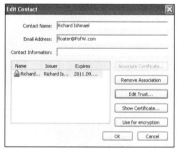

Figure 15.15 In the Edit Contact dialog box, choose the trusted identity, and click Edit Trust.

Figure 15.16 In the Import Contact Settings dialog box, you can specify that the identity should be used to verify signatures.

3. Click the Browse button.

A standard Open dialog box opens.

4. Choose the certificate file you want to import, and click OK.

Acrobat returns you to the Choose Contacts dialog box, which now lists the certificate you want to import (**Figure 15.13**).

5. Click the Import button.

Acrobat returns you to the Manage Trusted Identities dialog box, which now lists your new trusted signer (**Figure 15.14**).

You've now installed a new trusted identity, but you haven't specified what that identity is to be used for; specifically, you need to explicitly tell Acrobat that this identity can be used for signatures.

6. Click the newly installed trusted identity and then the Details button.

The Edit Contact dialog box opens (**Figure 15.15**), which presents a one-element list with the name of the certificate.

7. Click the name in the list and then the Edit Trust button.

The Import Contact Settings dialog box opens (**Figure 15.16**). This dialog box has check boxes that indicate the activities for which this identity can be trusted.

8. Choose the "Signatures and as a trusted root" and the "Certified documents" check boxes.

9. Click OK to return to the Edit Contact dialog box (Figure 15.15) and OK again to return to the Manage Trusted Identities dialog box.

10. Click the Close button to close the dialog box.

Your copy of Acrobat will now recognize signatures placed on a PDF page by the person whose certificate you imported.

IMPORTING A CERTIFICATE AS A TRUSTED IDENTITY

Signing a PDF Document

Having created your digital ID and sent certificates to the appropriate people, the actual signing of a document is pretty easy.

Once you've signed a PDF document, Acrobat saves the file in what is called an *increment-only* form. The contents of this type of PDF document cannot be removed from the file. New items can be added to the signed file, but Acrobat can always revert to the original, signed version of the document. This is what makes it possible to use a signed PDF file as a legal document: You can always see the document to which people affixed their signatures.

To sign a PDF document:

1. With the document open, choose Advanced > Sign & Certify > Place Signature.

   Acrobat reminds you how to place a signature on the page (**Figure 15.17**). This gets annoying after you've signed a few documents, so you should make use of the "Do not show this message again" check box.

2. Click OK in the reminder dialog box to return to your document, with the mouse pointer changed to a crosshairs.

3. Drag a rectangle on the page where you want the signature to go.

   The location of the signature is often a reserved place on a page within the document (**Figure 15.18**).

   When you release the mouse button, the Sign Document dialog box opens (**Figure 15.19**).

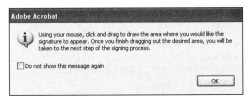

Figure 15.17 When you first sign a document, Acrobat presents a dialog box that reminds you of the procedure.

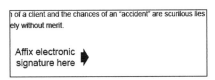

Figure 15.18 The document page will probably have a place reserved for your electronic signature.

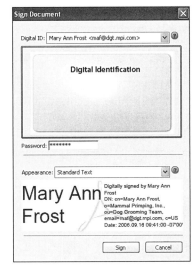

Figure 15.19 When you sign the document, Acrobat presents you with a dialog box that lets you specify the digital ID you want to use and to type the corresponding password.

of a client and the chances of an "accident" are scurrilous lies ly without merit.

| Affix electronic signature here | ➡ |  |

Figure 15.20 When you return to the document page, the signature appears as a bit of text with either your name in large print or a graphic.

4. Choose a digital ID from the Digital ID pop-up menu.

5. Type the ID's password into the Password field.

6. Choose an appearance from the Appearance pop-up menu.

There is initially only one appearance in this menu: Standard Text. You'll see how to create new appearances in the next section.

7. Click the Sign button.

Acrobat returns you to the document page, which now has the electronic signature placed on it (**Figure 15.20**).

✔ Tip

■ If the person who created the PDF document intended it to be signed (which is true for contracts and similar documents), then they will almost certainly place a signature field on the page, which eliminates a step or two in this process. We'll discuss signature fields later in this chapter.

SIGNING A PDF DOCUMENT

Creating a Signature Appearance

By default, the visible representation of a signature on a PDF page is a generic icon accompanied by a collection of text information, as in Figure 15.20. You can change the appearance of the signature, if you wish. Specifically, you can specify what information should be presented as text, and you can choose an image or other graphic that becomes part of the signature.

You do this by creating one or more named *appearances* in your Acrobat preferences. The appearance consists of a list of the text information and the image that should visually identify your signature on the page.

When you sign a document, one of the controls that appears in the Sign Document dialog box (Figure 15.19) is a pop-up menu of all the appearances available to your copy of Acrobat (**Figure 15.21**). Simply choose the appearance you want to use for the signature.

✔ Tip

- These visual marks don't make up the electronic signature itself. The actual signature is a wad of binary information that is embedded in the PDF file and isn't directly visible on the page. A signature's appearance specifies the details of a visible indication that a signature is placed on the page.

To create an appearance for your signatures:

1. On the Macintosh, choose Acrobat 8 > Preferences; in Windows, choose Edit > Preferences.

   The Preferences dialog box opens (**Figure 15.22**).

Figure 15.21 The Sign Document dialog box lets you choose an appearance to use with your signature.

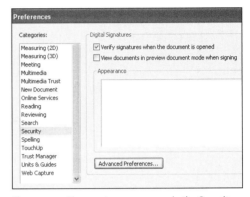

Figure 15.22 You create appearances in the Security Preferences.

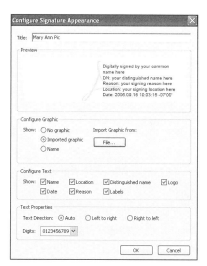

Figure 15.23 When you configure an appearance, you specify a graphic to use in your signatures and itemize what information should appear in the signature's text block.

Figure 15.24 The Configure Appearance dialog box presents a preview of what your signature looks like, based on the control settings.

Figure 15.25 Your new appearance is in the list on the Security Preferences pane.

Figure 15.26 When you sign a document, Acrobat applies the appearance you chose to the signature.

2. Choose Security in the Categories list on the left side of the dialog box.

3. Click the New button.

The Configure Signature Appearance dialog box opens (**Figure 15.23**).

4. Type a title for your appearance in the Title field at the top of the dialog box.

This name will appear in the pop-up menu when you sign a document.

5. If you want to have a picture appear as part of your signature, choose the "Imported graphic" radio button, and click the File button.

A standard Open dialog box opens, letting you choose the image, PDF, or other graphic file you want to use for your signature. Acrobat lets you use a wide variety of file types for your signature graphic, including PDF files, TIFFs, and JPEGs.

6. In the Configure Text section, choose the check boxes corresponding to the information you want to appear in the text part of your signature. I recommend selecting at least your name and the date.

The Preview in the dialog box reflects your choices (**Figure 15.24**).

7. Click OK to return to the Security Preferences, which now lists your new appearance (**Figure 15.25**). Click OK again to dismiss the Preferences dialog box.

Now, when you sign a PDF document, you can choose your appearance in the Sign Document dialog box, and the new signature is displayed on the page using your appearance details (**Figure 15.26**).

Creating a Signature Field

If you're creating a PDF file that contains a contract or other document that must be signed by the reader, you'll make things easier if you provide a *signature field* as part of the document. This is the electronic equivalent of a "sign here" line in a paper document; when the reader clicks this form field, it presents the Sign Document dialog box (Figure 15.19) so the reader can sign the document.

Having created your PDF document, you place a signature field on the page using the Signature Field tool in the Forms toolbar (**Figure 15.27**).

To create a signature field on a document page:

1. With the document open, choose the Signature Field tool in the Forms toolbar.

   The mouse cursor turns into a crosshairs.

2. Drag a rectangle on the page, indicating where the signature field should go (**Figure 15.28**).

   The Digital Signature Properties dialog box opens (**Figure 15.29**).

3. Click the General tab.

4. In the Tooltip field, type a phrase prompting readers to click the field when they're ready to sign the document. I suggest something like "Click here to digitally sign this document."

5. Click the Appearance tab.

6. Use these controls (**Figure 15.30**) to specify the color you want for the border and fill colors.

   Black for the border and white for the fill work well. This assumes you don't already have artwork for the field built into the page, in which case, you should choose None for these colors.

Figure 15.27 You create a signature field with the Signature Field tool on the Forms toolbar.

Figure 15.28 With the Signature Field tool selected, drag out a rectangle indicating the location of the signature field.

Figure 15.29 The General tab among the Digital Signature Properties lets you type in some tooltip text; the other controls can be safely ignored.

Figure 15.30 In the Appearance tab, specify the color and width of the field's border and fill.

CREATING A SIGNATURE FIELD

Figure 15.31 In the Signed tab, specify what should happen when a signature is fixed to the field.

Figure 15.32 When you return to the page, the field is visible as a rectangle with handles.

Figure 15.33 When you return to the Acrobat Hand tool, the mouse pointer becomes a pointing finger when it passes over the field. The tooltip text appears after a half-second.

7. Click the Signed tab.

Acrobat displays the controls that dictate what should happen when the user signs the document (**Figure 15.31**).

8. Choose the "Mark as read-only" radio button, and choose "All fields" in the pop-up menu, which ensures that no further changes can be made after the reader has signed the document,.

9. Click the Close button.

Acrobat returns you to the document page. The new signature field is visible as a rectangle with handles (**Figure 15.32**).

10. Reposition and resize the field by dragging the rectangle and its handles.

11. Click the Hand tool (or any other tool).

The new, functional signature field is visible as a rectangle with a small icon in the upper-left corner. When the mouse pointer moves over the field, it turns into a pointing finger; if you leave it over the field for a half-second, the tooltip text you specified appears (**Figure 15.33**). When the user clicks inside the field, the Sign Document dialog box opens so they can sign the document.

✔ Tip

■ In step 8, you specify that all the document's form fields should be locked when the document is signed. Alternatively, you can have only some of the fields locked, selecting them from the pop-up menu visible in Figure 15.31; you can have nothing in particular happen when the user signs the document; or you can have Acrobat execute a JavaScript when the document is signed. The most generally useful action is the one you specified: lock the document's form fields so no further changes can be made.

Validating a Signed Document

When you receive a signed document, you need to verify that the signature was placed on the page by the correct person. In Acrobat, this means verifying that the signature was placed on the page by someone who exists among your trusted identities. This process is referred to as *validating* the signature.

When you open a signed document, Acrobat automatically compares the digital ID of the signer with your trusted identities. If it finds a match, then Acrobat displays a checkmark icon within the signature's border, as in **Figure 15.34**.

This validation process happens automatically when you open the signed document. The only time you need to do anything special is if a signature fails to validate, indicated by a question mark icon in the signature graphic (Figure 15.34). In this case, you must try to validate the signature manually.

Figure 15.34 Acrobat attaches one of two icons to your signature. The icon at left means the signature was verified; the one at right indicates the signature is invalid.

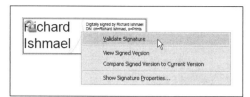

Figure 15.35 To validate a signature, right-click it, and choose Validate Signature.

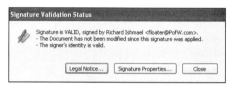

Figure 15.36 Acrobat will present you with a dialog box that tells you whether the signature is valid.

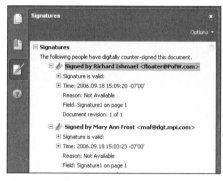

Figure 15.37 The Signatures navigation pane lists all the signatures in the current document.

To validate a signature manually:

◆ Right-click the signature, and choose Validate Signature from the contextual menu (**Figure 15.35**).

Acrobat attempts to validate the signature and displays a dialog box reporting the result (**Figure 15.36**).

If a signature is invalid, the reporting dialog box tells you why. Validation usually fails because the signer isn't among your trusted identities. You need to contact the signer, get a certificate from that person, and then import that certificate into your copy of Acrobat. Then you can revalidate the signature.

You can validate all of the signatures in a document using the Signatures navigation pane (**Figure 15.37**). This pane lists all of the signatures in the current document, together with an icon indicating whether each signature is valid.

To validate all signatures in a document:

1. Click the Signatures navigation pane icon to make the pane visible.

2. In the Options menu, choose Validate All Signatures (**Figure 15.38**).

   Acrobat attempts to validate all of the document's signatures, placing a Valid or Invalid icon (Figure 15.34) next to each.

A signed document can still be changed using the touch-up and commenting tools. However, even if extensive changes have been made to the document since its signing, it's always possible to revert to the document as it was at signing.

To revert to the original signed version of a document:

◆ Right-click the signature in which you're interested, and choose View Signed Version (Figure 15.38).

   The document reverts to the signed version. You're looking at the document exactly as it was when it was signed.

✔ Tip

■ You should also try out Compare Signed Version to Current Version in the contextual menu in Figure 15.38. It shows you the signed and current versions of the document side by side, with the differences highlighted. Quite cool.

Figure 15.38 Using the Options menu in the Signatures navigation pane, you can validate all the signatures in the document.

VALIDATING A SIGNED DOCUMENT

CONVERTING
PAPER TO PDF

We have spent this book discussing the wonderful things you can do with PDF documents; however, most of the important official documents we all receive are printed on paper. Professionals are particularly wedded to paper: contracts, estimates, invoices, are most frequently distributed as paper documents. Until relatively recently, even Adobe insisted that some of their developer applications be printed, signed, and faxed back to them; PDF files weren't accepted. For that matter, most companies have many years' worth of paper stored in warehouses, documenting all of their past transactions and business.

What if you want to store these documents on your disk or fill them out electronically? You'll scan the paper and then store or otherwise deal with the scanned image. Because Acrobat can open image files, automatically converting them to PDF, scanned paper documents can be treated entirely as PDF files.

In this chapter, you'll see what you can do with a scanned paper document. Acrobat provides tools for conveniently filling out scanned paper forms and for converting scanned text into searchable, real text.

This chapter assumes you've already scanned the paper document with which you're working.

Typing on a Paper Form

If you scan a paper form that you need to fill out, (or, for that matter, if you receive a PDF-format form that doesn't have form fields), you have a document that looks like a form but, in an Acrobat sense, isn't one. The lines and boxes where you're supposed to write your information are just graphic objects, not interactive form fields that collect information (**Figure 16.1**).

You can lay form fields on top of the scanned pages, but if the form is something you need to fill out only once and then forget about, placing form fields on the page seems like unnecessary work. What you'd really like to do is type your responses on top of the page contents, exactly as though you were printing or typing on a paper page.

The Typewriter tool allows you to do exactly that. This is a truly useful little gadget for those of us who prefer to do everything electronically if at all possible. Every time you click the page with the Typewriter tool, you get a blinking cursor, which lets you type text onto the page (**Figure 16.2**). The tool emulates typing with a typewriter (remember those?), so the text is always in Courier.

This makes it easy to fill in one-off forms that you'll never see or bother with again. The form you fill in can be emailed to another person or, of course, printed and faxed. The typed-on form can be opened with Acrobat 5 or later.

The Typewriter tool is most easily used through the Typewriter toolbar (**Figure 16.3**).

✔ Tip

■ Although here we're discussing the Typewriter tool with regard to scanned paper documents, you can use it to type onto any PDF document.

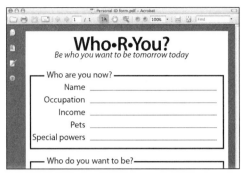

Figure 16.1 When you scan a paper form, the result may look like a form, but it isn't, in an Acrobat sense. The lines where you type your data are merely lines, not Acrobat form fields.

Figure 16.2 The Typewriter tool lets you type text on top of the PDF page, exactly like typing on a paper form.

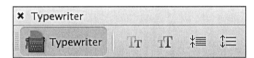

Figure 16.3 The Typewriter toolbar has the Typewriter tool, the decrease and increase text size buttons, and the decrease and increase text spacing buttons.

Figure 16.4 Having typed your text, you can click it with the Hand, Select, or Typewriter tool to get a border with handles. These let you resize and reposition the text.

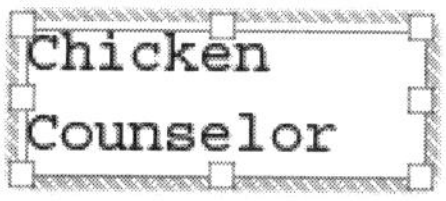

Figure 16.5 If you shorten the text's border too much, the text will wrap itself into multiple lines.

To type form responses onto a PDF page:

1. With the document open, choose the Typewriter tool from the Typewriter toolbox.

   The mouse pointer turns into an I-beam.

2. Click the page where you want to type your text.

   Presumably, this will be above or in some graphic element on the page, such as a line or a box.

3. Type your text.

   If you click the typewritten text with the Typewriter, Selection, or Hand tool, Acrobat places a rectangle with handles around the text (**Figure 16.4**). You can now reposition the text by dragging the rectangle around the page. You can resize the bounding box of the text by dragging the handles; if you make the box too narrow to accommodate the text, Acrobat wraps it into multiple lines (**Figure 16.5**).

✔ Tips

- You can edit your typewritten text by double-clicking it with either the Hand or the Typewriter tool.

- The Typewriter toolbar (Figure 16.3) also has buttons to change the point size or the spacing between typewritten lines. Click the typewritten text to select it, and then click the button.

TYPING ON PAPER FORM

Creating a Searchable Image

When you scan a paper document—a contract, say—the result is a bitmapped picture of the original text and graphics (**Figure 16.6**). Although it looks like pages of text, there is, in fact, no text there.

If you're simply reading the document, this doesn't matter; the eye doesn't care if it's looking at text or a picture of text. However, if you're hoping to use common computer text functions with the document—in particular, if you want to be able to search the document for words or phrases—then a picture of the text won't do. You must have pages of actual text.

Acrobat has a built-in Optical Character Recognition (OCR) function that can analyze an image and convert the picture of the text into real text that can be searched.

The appearance of the page remains that of the scanned text; the searchable text occupies an invisible layer that coincides with the scanned text. This preserves the original appearance and relieves Acrobat of having to guess at the font, point size, and other characteristics of the original text. This combination of an image and an invisible text layer is called a *searchable image*.

In a searchable image, all of Acrobat's text-related tools and features (in particular, the Find feature and the Select tool) work as usual, applying themselves to the invisible text layer. Thus, in addition to searching for text, you can copy and paste text from the PDF page into another application (**Figure 16.7**).

To create a searchable image PDF file:

1. With the image file open in Acrobat, select Document > OCR Text Recognition > Recognize Text Using OCR.

   The Recognize Text dialog box opens (**Figure 16.8**).

Figure 16.6 When you scan a paper page, the result may look like text, but it's really a bitmapped picture of the text.

Figure 16.7 In a searchable image, the original bitmap image is unchanged, but there is an invisible text layer whose text can be selected, searched for, copied, and pasted. Here, we've apparently selected some bitmapped text with the Selection tool; in fact, we've selected the underlying real text.

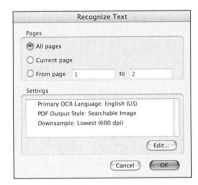

Figure 16.8 The Recognize Text dialog box lets you specify the pages that should be converted. Clicking the Edit button lets you specify the details of the conversion.

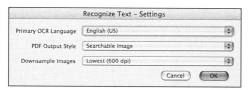

Figure 16.9 The Recognize Text-Settings dialog box lets you specify the language and style you want for the OCR process. You can also specify down-sampling resolution, but you shouldn't.

Figure 16.10 The PDF Output Style menu lets you specify what kind of file should result from the text recognition.

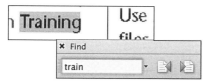

Figure 16.11 Having converted your document to a searchable image, you can search for words and phrases within the document.

2. Choose which pages you want Acrobat to convert: all pages, the current page, or a specific range of pages.

   You'll probably nearly always choose "All pages."

3. In the Settings section of the dialog box, click the Edit button.

   The Recognize Text - Settings dialog box opens (**Figure 16.9**).

4. In the PDF Output Style pop-up menu, choose Searchable Image (**Figure 16.10**).

5. If necessary, choose the language of the text in the Primary OCR Language pop-up menu.

6. Click OK to return to the Recognize Text dialog box, and click OK once more to have Acrobat convert your document.

   Acrobat analyzes your pages' bitmaps and creates the invisible text layer. When Acrobat is finished converting your document, the pages look unchanged; but if you search for a phrase, Acrobat can find it and highlight it (**Figure 16.11**).

✔ Tips

- The PDF Output Style pop-up menu (Figure 16.10) also presents two additional choices: Searchable Image (Exact), which is the same as Searchable Image but uses a more sophisticated (and slower) OCR method; and Formatted Text & Graphics, which we'll discuss in the next section. In the context of this discussion, choosing Searchable Image is a good compromise between OCR speed and accuracy.

- OCR works best with a 300 dpi monochrome (1-bit, black and white) scan. I find it works acceptably with 150 dpi scans, as well. Adobe claims that 72 dpi is adequate, but you'll find some mistakes in the character recognition with such a coarse bitmap.

CREATING A SEARCHABLE IMAGE

Converting a Scan to Text and Graphics

In the previous section, we showed how Acrobat creates a special, invisible text layer beneath a scanned bitmap. This leaves the scanned image visually unchanged but lets you search for phrases in the scanned text.

Keeping the page as a bitmap maintains the look and feel of the page; however, you cannot edit the text, and zooming in on the text makes it look jagged and unpleasant.

If you'd like to convert your scanned pages into something that can be edited using the TouchUp tools, you need to convert your scan to a combination of actual text and line art, discarding the bitmap altogether. You can do this by converting the scanned page to Text & Graphics.

Once you've converted the document, you can do anything to the pages' text or graphics that is possible in Acrobat: search, edit, reposition, and so on. The disadvantage is that Acrobat often can't match the text's original font and picks a substitute from among your system fonts; thus, the appearance of your text will probably change (**Figure 16.12**).

Figure 16.12 Converting your image to text and graphics makes the text smooth but usually changes the font. Compare this with Figure 16.6.

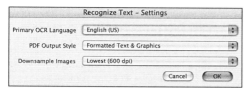

Figure 16.13 Select "Formatted Text & Graphics" in the PDF Output Style menu.

To convert a scanned document to text and graphics:

1. With the image file open in Acrobat, select Document > OCR Text Recognition > Recognize Text Using OCR. Acrobat will display the Recognize Text dialog box (Figure 16.8).

2. Choose which pages you want Acrobat to convert: all pages, the current page, or a specific range of pages.

You'll probably nearly always choose All pages.

3. In the Settings section of the dialog box, click the Edit button.

The Recognize Text-Settings dialog box opens (**Figure 16.13**).

4. In the PDF Output Style pop-up menu, choose Formatted Text & Graphics.

5. If necessary, choose the language of the text in the Primary OCR Language pop-up menu.

6. Click OK to return to the Recognize Text dialog box and click OK again to have Acrobat convert your document.

✔ Tip

■ Converting a scan to text and graphics requires a higher-resolution image than creating a searchable image (the previous topic). A 300 dpi monochrome scan is best, and text recognition is still very good at 150 dpi. However, Acrobat has less success identifying the text's font at lower resolution. Also, if your document has small text (9 points or smaller), you should probably scan at a resolution higher than 300 dpi.

Correcting OCR Suspects

When Acrobat converts your scanned document into text, it must look at the bitmap for every character on the scanned page and identify the text character it represents. Sometimes Acrobat can't decide what character a little piece of bitmap is supposed to be. This is referred to as an *OCR suspect;* Acrobat guesses the character's identity, but it may guess wrong.

When this happens, Acrobat leaves that character on the page as a bitmap (**Figure 16.14**).

You can step through Acrobat's list of suspects for a converted document and correct its character identification. For each suspect, Acrobat shows you the original bitmap and its guess as to the character it represents, and gives you a chance to accept it or change it.

You should always make this the final step in converting a document from scanned material to PDF.

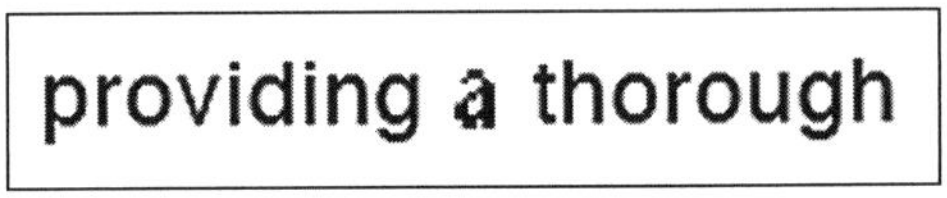

providing a thorough

Figure 16.14 The bitmapped *a* in the middle of this text is an OCR suspect, a bit of the scanned page that Acrobat wasn't sure how to convert to text.

Figure 16.15 When you correct OCR suspects, Acrobat highlights them one at a time, allowing you to make a decision as to the text the suspect should represent.

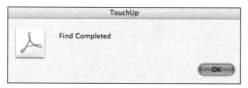

Figure 16.16 Acrobat tells you when you're finished cycling through the OCR suspects.

To correct OCR suspects:

1. With the converted document open, select Document > OCR Text Recognition > Find First OCR Suspect.

   Acrobat highlights the first suspect and opens the Find Element dialog box (**Figure 16.15**).

2. For each suspect, do one of the following:

   ▲ If the bitmap isn't a text character, click the Not Text button.

   ▲ If the bitmap is a text character, change the text in the Suspect text box to the proper character (if necessary), and click Accept and Find.

   ▲ If you don't want to make a decision just now (perhaps it's not clear even to you what the bitmap is), then click the Find Next button.

   In all three cases, Acrobat moves to the next suspect. Repeat until Acrobat tells you there are no more suspects (**Figure 16.16**).

3. Click the Close button.

✔ Tip

■ Remember that if the document you are correcting is a searchable image, you won't see any changes on the page when you correct a bit of text. Your corrections are applied to the invisible text layer.

FOR MORE
INFORMATION

Acrobat has accumulated around it a large collection of resources might be useful if you look for information beyond what's covered in this book. These resources will all be busily updating themselves to accommodate Acrobat 8 and, by the time you read this, all of them will probably have much to say about the new version of Acrobat.

Books

Following are some Acrobat books that I use and admire, presented in no particular order.

◆ *Adobe Acrobat 8.0 Classroom in a Book* (Adobe Creative Team, Adobe Press, 2007) This is Adobe's official tutorial on how to use Acrobat. It's well written and complete, if occasionally a bit dense for a novice.

◆ *Adobe Acrobat 8 How-Tos* (Donna L. Baker, Adobe Press, 2007)

◆ *Adobe Acrobat 8 in the Office* (Donna L. Baker, Adobe Press, 2007) Ms. Baker writes very good "how to" books; I can recommend anything she writes.

◆ *Extending Acrobat Forms with JavaScript* (John Deubert, Adobe Press, 2003) Written by yours truly. If you want a non-programmer's introduction to programming Acrobat using JavaScript, this is the only book available.

◆ *Adobe Acrobat 8 PDF Bible* (Ted Padova, Wiley, 2007) Mr. Padova is the master of the Bible series books. This thick volume covers all of Acrobat in vast detail. It is well worth having, though its size can be a bit daunting.

◆ **Acumen Journal** (John Deubert) This is my free, more-or-less-bimonthly periodical. Each issue has an article on some facet of advanced Acrobat use. Recent articles include *Setting Up Form Auto-Completion* and *Adding Menu Items to Acrobat with JavaScript*. You can find it at the Acumen Training Web site: www.acumentraining.com.

Web Resources

There are countless Web sites devoted to tricks, tips, and discussions regarding Acrobat. A Web search will serve up the names of literally tens of thousands of such sites. The ones I can recommend as being particularly useful are:

- **PlanetPDF.com** This is a rich Web site filled with white papers, forums, online classes, book reviews, and many other resources for people working with PDF. The range of expertise to which it caters runs the gamut from novice through power user to experienced plug-in programmer.

- **PDFZone.com** Very similar to PlanetPDF.com, this site may not offer quite as much variety, but many people find its layout more user friendly. (I visit both sites frequently.)

- **www.AcumenTraining.com** My own Web site has a large collection of sample files, most of them related to articles in the *Acumen Journal.*

- **comp.text.pdf** This is representative of the dozen or so newsgroups that address Acrobat and PDF issues. It's worth perusing periodically to look at people's questions and the corresponding answers and discussions. Of course, you can post your own questions, as well.

WEB RESOURCES

INDEX

INDEX

INDEX

INDEX

INDEX

INDEX

GET UP AND RUNNING QUICKLY!

For more than 15 years, the practical approach to the best-selling *Visual QuickStart Guide* series from Peachpit Press has helped millions of readers—from developers to designers to systems administrators and more—get up to speed on all sorts of computer programs. Now with select titles in full color for the first time, *Visual QuickStart Guide* books provide an even easier and more enjoyable way for readers to learn about new technology through task-based instruction, friendly prose, and visual explanations.

Task-Based
Information is broken down into concise, one- and two-page tasks to help you get right to work.

Visual
Hundreds of screen shots illustrate the steps and show you the best way to do them.

Step by Step
Numbered, easy-to-follow instructions guide you through each task.

Tips
Lots of helpful tips are highlighted throughout the book.

Quick Reference
Tabs on each page identify the task, making it easy to find what you're looking for.

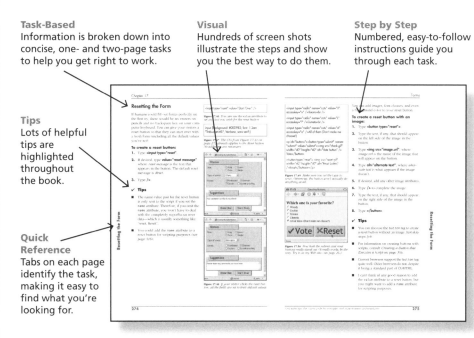